STRANGE
BUT
TRUE
MILITARY FACTS

STRANGE BUT TRUE
MILITARY FACTS

STEVE CRAWFORD

METRO BOOKS
NEW YORK

ISBN: 978-1-4351-2435-6

Editorial and Design
Windmill Books Ltd.
First Floor, 9-17 St. Albans Place
London N1 ONX

Metro Books
122 Fifth Avenue
New York, NY 10011

Editors: Dennis Cove, Peter Darman
Designers: Tim Mayer, Theresa Maynard, Geoff Ward
Production Director: Alastair Gourlay
Senior Managing Editor: Timothy Cooke
Editorial Director: Lindsey Lowe
Creative Director: Jeni Child
Design Manager: David Poole
Index: Indexing Specialists (UK) Ltd.

Printed and bound in China

1 3 5 7 9 10 8 6 4 2

Picture credits:
All images The Robert Hunt Library, except:
Getty Images/Hulton: 48 (bottom)
TopFoto: 51

Front cover image:
Prince George, Duke of Cambridge,
commander-in-chief of the British Army 1856–95

CONTENTS

INTRODUCTION

Warfare is one of mankind's most popular activities. Since earliest times, rulers and kingdoms have raised and organized armies and then set them upon neighbors. The thousands of years spent practising the art of organized killing has resulted in a great body of knowledge being amassed about how warfare should be conducted. This knowledge has been codified into what is termed the "rules of war." They are supposed to be set in stone, but as the chapters in this book illustrate, once the fighting begins the rule book is often the first casualty, to be replaced by the weird, eccentric, and frankly bizarre.

GENERALS
It's not entirely the fault of generals, and even the great Field Marshal

Marlborough's cavalry in action—forced to use steel because they had few bullets.

The Duke of Marlborough, the victor of Blenheim.

Helmuth von Moltke (1800–91) of the Prussian Army said: "I never plan beyond the first battle." That is because once battle is joined, events can rapidly spiral out of anyone's control, the more so if prior planning has been poor or non-existent. Add on top the eccentricities of commanders, and the result can be mayhem. Marshal Gebhard Blücher (1742–1819), for example, was a superb battlefield leader but was also insane. Even such greats as the John Churchill, 1st Duke of Marlborough (1650–1722), the famed victor of the Battle of Blenheim (1704), had their quirks. Churchill favored having his cavalry close with the enemy to use "cold steel." To encourage them to use their swords, he kept his cavalry short of ammunition so that they would not be tempted to stand off from the enemy and use their firearms!

THE POOR BLOODY INFANTRY
The lot of infantrymen has also rarely been a happy one. Going back to the eighteenth and nineteenth centuries,

foot soldiers were not only dressed in colorful, uncomfortable uniforms, they also wore white crossbelts on their chests, which, as well as looking neat, also provided a superb aiming point for enemy soldiers. And it got even better for the opposition when infantry regiments stood their soldiers shoulder-to-shoulder on the battlefield, and several ranks deep. The result was surely carnage. Actually, it wasn't, at least not all of the time. Fortunately, or unfortunately depending on what side you were on, infantrymen were armed with the musket. This weapon, which appears in Chapter 7, was one of the most useless firearms ever invented. So much so that opposing armies had to get really close to each other to inflict any damage. Its shortcomings didn't prevent it remaining in service around the world for 200 years, though.

WEAPONS

Weapons have always been a lottery as far as armies are concerned. No one really knows if they are going to work properly until the fighting starts. Likewise, mechanical engines are always prone to difficulties, especially in battlefield conditions. But it must have been a disappointment to the British when they sent their tanks to France to fight the Germans in 1940, during World War II. Of those tanks lost, only 25 percent fell victim to enemy action; the rest were due to mechanical breakdowns. Russian tanks were far more rugged (though not always wholly reliable), and so a higher proportion made it onto the battlefield. Sadly, most did not make it off it. In World War II the Red Army deployed 108,700 tanks. Of these, a staggering 76.8 percent—83,500— were lost in combat.

One of the 83,500 Red Army tanks destroyed during World War II.

MILITARY BUDGETS

By the twentieth century, airpower had become a major component of warfare, with associated costs. The production costs for the U.S. B-2 "stealth" bomber comes in at over $2 billion per aircraft. It was designed to penetrate the sophisticated air defenses of the Soviet Union, though the USSR no longer exists and the B-2 doesn't really have a role. This is just one example of many strange but true facts that litter the annals of military history.

THE ART OF WAR

Warfare is one of mankind's most popular pastimes, having been indulged in since ancient times. And though it is usually a serious business, it also has its more bizarre moments.

FACT FILE

Sunday is supposed to be a day of peace, yet during World War II several offensives were launched on a Sunday.

- September 3, 1939—Britain declares war on Germany for invading Poland and starts World War II.

- June 22, 1941—Germany invades the Soviet Union.

- December 7, 1941—sneaky Japanese attack on the U.S. naval base at Pearl Harbor.

- November 9, 1942—Allied amphibious invasion of North Africa.

- September 17, 1944—Allied Operation Market Garden in Holland.

- April 1, 1945—U.S. invasion of the Japanese island of Okinawa.

- July 1, 1945—Allied invasion of Balikpapan, Borneo.

CRAZY CONFLICTS

Some wars have arisen thanks to the strangest, almost incredible, set of causes.

THE WAR OF THE BUCKET

(1352): Modena's soldiers invaded Bologna in Italy, killing thousands of citizens and capturing an old oak bucket (right). Bologna went to war to recapture its bucket. The fighting lasted for 12 years and cost thousands of lives, but Bologna never recovered its bucket.

THE RUSSO-SPANISH WAR

(1799–1801): The exiled Knights of Malta, having sought refuge in Russia, elected Tsar Paul I to be their Grand Master. Other knights, having found refuge in Spain, elected one of their brethren. Tsar Paul—totally mad—declared war. No one seems to have been killed in this conflict over an island which neither side possessed.

THE FLAGSTAFF WAR (1845):

The British erected a flagstaff in the town of Kororareka, New Zealand. Hone Heke, a chief of the natives, chopped it down, and a second and a third. Violence erupted when a fourth was erected. Heke and his tribe descended on the town, butchering townsfolk. The resulting war lasted 10 months. The British were victorious, but didn't erect another flagstaff.

THE PIG WAR (1859): Fought

between U.S. and British authorities over the boundary separating the United States and British North America, near Vancouver. The specific area in dispute was the San Juan Islands. The war was triggered by the shooting of a pig, which was the war's only "casualty."

THE WAR OF THE STRAY DOG

(1925): This broke out when a Greek soldier allegedly ran after his dog, which had strayed across the border into Bulgaria. The border was guarded by Bulgarian sentries, and one of them shot the Greek soldier. The Greeks then sent soldiers into Bulgaria. Bulgaria ordered its troops to provide only token resistance. Over 50 people were killed before Greece withdrew.

THE FOOTBALL WAR (1969):

This was a four-day war between El Salvador and Honduras. Existing tensions between the two countries coincided with rioting during the second North American qualifying round for the 1970 FIFA World Cup. On July 14, 1969, the Salvadoran Army launched an attack against Honduras, withdrawing in August.

LONGEST WARS

118 YEARS: THE PUNIC WARS, a series of three wars fought between Rome and Carthage from 264 to 146 B.C. The conflict resulted in the destruction of Carthage.

116 YEARS: THE HUNDRED YEARS' WAR (1337–1453) between England and France. All the major battles occurred in France or at sea.

30 YEARS: THE THIRTY YEARS' WAR (1618–48), a religious conflict fought in central Europe that resulted in the extermination of a third of Germany's population.

29 YEARS: THE VIETNAM WAR (1946–75), the defeat of France, the United States, and South Vietnam at the hands of the communist North Vietnamese and their allies.

27 YEARS: THE PELOPONNESIAN WAR (431–404 B.C.), between Athens and its empire and the Peloponnesian League, led by Sparta. The latter was victorious.

Oddballs

In April 1986, the Council of the Isles of Scilly, 30 miles (48 km) west of Land's End, Great Britain, concluded a peace treaty with Holland. This ended a state of war that had existed between the two since 1651, when the Dutch got tired of having their ships victimized by Scillian "false-lighters," who would erect and set fire to decoy beacons to lure ships onto rocks, to be plundered by the wreckers.

SHORTEST WARS

24 DAYS: The Georgian-Armenian War was an inconclusive border war fought in 1918 between Georgia and the Democratic Republic of Armenia.

14 DAYS: The Serbo-Bulgarian War in 1885 resulted in a Bulgarian victory.

13 DAYS: In the 1971 Indo-Pakistan War, the Indians won, resulting in the creation of Bangladesh.

6 DAYS: The Six Day War, 1967, with Israel fighting Egypt, Syria, Jordan, and Iraq. Israeli aircraft destroyed the Arab air forces on the first day.

45 MINUTES: The Anglo-Zanzibar War between Great Britain and Zanzibar on August 27, 1896. The British Royal Navy destroyed the palace of Sultan Hamad bin Thuwaini, including his harem (rotters).

FACT FILE

- -

The 1914 Christmas Truce, World War I

By Christmas 1914 the soldiers on the Western Front were totally exhausted. At dawn on December 25, the British in trenches around the Belgian city of Ypres heard carols ringing out from the opposing German positions, and then spied Christmas trees being placed along the front of the German trenches. Slowly, lines of German soldiers climbed out of their trenches and advanced to the halfway point of No-Man's Land, where they called on the British to join them. The two sides met in the middle, exchanged gifts, talked, and played games of football.

FACT FILE

- -

Curious facts about the Roman Army

• The smallest unit in a legion was the tent group (*contubernium*)—eight men who shared a tent, a mule, and cooking equipment.

• Tent groups were organized into a century (which had 80 rather than 100 men). Six centuries made up a cohort; 10 cohorts a legion.

• Wounded soldiers wore spiders' webs as wound dressings. The sticky silk helped the skin to knit together. Tucking a bundle of herbs into the bandage was another trick—it killed germs.

• Roman soldiers were tattooed on the arms with their legion's logo, the ink being applied using sharp tools. Tattooing was done so that deserters could be easily identified.

ANCIENT ANTICS

Eunuchs were very popular in ancient times, particularly in China. And some eunuchs had successful military careers, including Tong Guan of China's Northern Song Dynasty, who controlled the emperor's armies for 20 years. And then there was Narses (478–573), a Byzantine general under Justinian I (482–565), who commanded the imperial bodyguard.

MILITARY MADNESS

The ancient Chinese (right) were very particular when it came to observing the rules of military etiquette.

In 638 B.C., for example, the Chinese Duke of Sung refused to attack an enemy army as it was crossing a river, believing such an act to be unchivalrous. Afterward, he boasted that he had preserved his honor, which indeed he had. Unfortunately, he also lost the battle.

Similarly, in 554 B.C., an invasion of the Chinese state of Qi was called off after the attackers learned that the ruler of Qi had just died, and deemed it inappropriate to continue the war.

And during the Eastern Zhou period of Chinese history (770–221 B.C.), battles allegedly were fought according to rigid rules of etiquette, with personnel strictly prohibited from engaging or killing opponent who were of a different social rank.

STRANGE SIEGES

MASADA (73): When Jewish zealots took refuge on a high outcrop by the Dead Sea, they were besieged by a Roman legion under Flavius Silva. The Romans built a massive assault ramp, upon which they mounted a siege tower equipped with a battering ram. But the 960 defenders took their own lives before the final assault.

NISHAPUR (1221): Having captured the Persian city of Nishapur in 1221, the Mongols slaughtered every inhabitant and then neatly arranged the heads of the slain in separate piles for men, women, and children. They also killed all the dogs, cats, cows, hogs, and other animals.

LUXEMBOURG (1463): When Philip the Good of Burgundy (1396–1467) captured the town in 1463, his soldiers observed excellent discipline while he went to offer prayers of thanksgiving in the local cathedral. Afterward, at his signal, the troops sacked the town.

FACT FILE

History's longest sieges

When (A.D.)	Where	How long
193–96	Byzantium	3 years
1992–96	Sarajevo	4 years
1267–73	Xiangyang (China)	6 years
1570–80	Ishiyama Honganji (Japan)	10 years
1648–69	Candia (Crete)	21 years

POLTAVA (1709): Tsar Peter the Great (1672–1725) communicated with the besieged garrison of Poltava by inserting messages in hollow cannon shells, which were fired back and forth over the heads of the besieging Swedes.

NAPLES (1734): When Duke Charles of Parma's Spanish forces besieged the Austrian-held Castel Nuovo in Naples in 1734, he was careful not to inflict undue harm on the city, which he intended to rule as king. One observer wrote: "The besiegers ... make signs with a handkerchief when they prepare to fire and they warn the inhabitants to return to their houses."

Oddballs

Wait till the moat freezes, then attack.

Water can be a major obstacle to an attacker, though only above freezing. In 1511, for example, the troops of Pope Julius II stormed the city of Mirandola in mid-winter by attacking across its frozen moat. And on the morning of January 23, 1795, a Lieutenant Colonel Lahure of the French Army led a squadron of hussars and an infantry company across thick sea ice around the Texel in Holland, to successfully capture the entire ice-bound Dutch Navy.

HORSEFLESH

Horses have been the battle companions of soldiers since earliest times, and they have suffered most cruelly at their masters' hands, dying of neglect, injuries, starvation, and the weather. To give an example of this suffering, of the 187,121 horses that Napoleon took with him on his invasion of Russia in June 1812, only some 1,600 survived the campaign. Over 100 years later, in 1941–45, another Russian campaign witnessed similar losses in horseflesh. In World War II, the Germans lost an average of 1,000 horses a day during

their campaign on the Eastern Front: 75 percent in combat, 17 percent to heart failure, and 8 percent to disease, exposure, and starvation.

MILITARY MADNESS

Until relatively recently, mules have been essential to armies for the movement of supplies, especially in inhospitable terrain. Though beasts of burden, they could often be cantankerous toward their masters. Peggy, for example, was a British Army mule in Italy in World War II. *Time* magazine printed her epitaph: "In memory of Peggy, who in her lifetime kicked one brigadier, two colonels, four majors, ten captains, twenty-four lieutenants, forty-two sergeants, sixty corporals, 436 other ranks, and one bomb."

Famous American Civil War individuals and the horses they rode

Belle Boyd	*Fleeter*
Major General William B. Bate	*Black Hawk*
Major General Patrick R. Cleburne	*Dixie*
Lieutenant General Richard S. Ewell	*Rifle*
Nathan Bedford Forrest	*King Philip*
Stonewall Jackson	*Old Sorrel*
General Albert S. Johnston	*Fire-eater*
General Robert E. Lee (right)	*Traveller*
Lieutenant General U. S. Grant	*Cincinnati*
Major General George B. McClellan	*Kentuck*
Brigadier General George G. Meade	*Baldy*
Colonel Philip Sheridan	*Aldebaron*

FACT FILE

Napoleonic cavalry mounts

Most Napoleonic armies preferred animals of about 15 hands
2 inches at the shoulder (1.6 m), weighing 990–1,1100 lb
(450–500 kg), heavier for cuirassiers (big men who wore
breastplates and helmets). Horses were usually bought at five
years of age, and saw 12 years of service. For pulling artillery
pieces and wagons, big, sturdy horses such as Percherons were
much sought after. Mares or geldings were preferred, as stallions
easily became uncontrollable around mares in season.

WAR AND PROSTITUTES

When not fighting, soldiers are renowned for gambling or hiring prostitutes. Between May and July 1567, for example, the Spanish general the Duke of Alba raised an army of 10,000 men in Naples. Attached to it were 2,000 courtesans. A hundred years later, the normal complement of an infantry company in the Spanish Army (right) was 75–100 soldiers and 3–8 prostitutes.

On October 28, 1914, the German ship *Emden* sank the Russian cruiser *Zhemchug*, which had no men on watch. Her entire crew were below decks entertaining 60 prostitutes.

FACT FILE

Punishments for prostitutes

• Prostitutes have often faced severe penalties for plying their trade. In 100, the Teutons, a Germanic tribe, would punish anyone caught working as a prostitute by suffocating them in excrement.

• An eighteenth-century French prostitute could be spared any punishment if she was willing to join the opera.

• In the seventeenth century, harlots caught in a military camp often had their noses slit as a "minor" punishment. (Curiously, as an aside, in modern-day Uruguay, a husband who catches his spouse in bed with another man is given an option under the current law. He has the right to kill both the wayward wife and her lover—or he can choose to slice off his wife's nose and castrate her lover.)

*Odd**balls***

Victory Girls was the name euphemistically given to women of less-than-pure morals who made themselves available to servicemen on leave in the United States in World War II. Many were married to other servicemen overseas. Many more were merely single girls attempting to cope with the shortage of eligible males.

COMFORT BATTALIONS

The Japanese Army of World War II had so-called "comfort battalions." It is estimated that 100,000–200,000 girls and women were conscripted as comfort women, essentially forced into prostitution. The majority of the women were from China, Korea, and Japan, but others came from the Philippines, Taiwan, Thailand, Vietnam, Singapore, the Dutch East Indies, and other Japanese-occupied countries and regions. There were around 2,000 centers in the Japanese Empire, where as many as 200,000 Korean, Chinese, Japanese, Filipino, Taiwanese, Burmese, Indonesian, Dutch, and Australian women were interned. Japanese authorities hoped that by providing easily accessible prostitutes and sexual slaves, the morale and ultimately the military effectiveness of Japanese soldiers would be improved. Many comfort women, when they had outlived their usefulness, were shot by their captors. To date the Japanese have expressed no regret for comfort battalions.

VENEREAL DISEASE

Soldiers and armies have always suffered from venereal disease (VD). Reducing VD cases is a problem that senior commanders have to wrestle with, often being forced to find unusual solutions.

THE AMERICAN CIVIL WAR

There were high rates of venereal disease in both armies, chiefly syphilis and gonorrhea. There were no antibiotics available, and some of the "cures" were almost worse than the disease. Mercury, zinc, and other substances were used, usually with poor results. Mercury had dangerous side effects, including hallucinations, kidney failure, and even insanity.

U.S. Army Provost Marshal Lieutenant Colonel George Spaulding established a system of prostitute licensing in Nashville. For the first time in American history, there was legalized prostitution—prostitutes could obtain a license for $5.00. They had to be examined for disease every 7–10 days. Those who passed got a certificate of "soundness." If she didn't pass, a prostitute would be sent to a special hospital—a facility funded by a special 50 cents tax on the women themselves. It was a success. Disease rates went down, and it was noted that a "better class" of prostitutes came to the city, drawn by the legalization and the relatively good health care provided.

WORLD WAR II

In Burma, some historians believe that British troops deliberately tried to contract VD before leaving for the front in order to be evacuated back to India. Indeed, India recorded the highest VD rate during the war, rising to nearly 80 cases per 1,000 troops by 1945.

MONTY, THE LOVE GENERAL

British General Bernard Montgomery (above) did not drink or smoke. During World War II, he was almost dismissed as a divisional commander in 1940 when he issued an order that his men were authorized to use approved brothels in order to avoid venereal disease. Montgomery survived, though he was subsequently nicknamed the "General of Love."

FACT FILE

Venereal disease in the U.S. Army since 1829

The U.S. Army has kept statistics on venereal disease in its ranks since the late 1820s.

Period	Situation	Rate
1829–38	Peace	60
1840–46	Peace	70
1846–48	Mexican War	90
1849–54	Peace	70
1861–65	Civil War	82
1880–90	Peace	83
1895	Peace	74
1897	Peace	84
1917–18	World War I	87
1941–45	World War II	49
1950–53	Korea	146
1965–72	Vietnam	325
1990–91	Persian Gulf War	n/a

Rate is the number of cases per 1,000 men. It does not represent the percentage of men with a venereal condition, since one man can be infected several times.

BATTLES, NUMBERS, & MYTHS

Battles are the crucible of war, where deeds great and terrible are performed. But the clash of armies can often give rise to myths and falsehoods, which over the course of time become accepted as fact.

EARLIEST BATTLES IN HISTORY
The Battle of Megiddo (1457 B.C.) took place during a rebellion against Egyptian Pharaoh Thutmose III. It was fought between the Egyptians and a large Canaanite coalition under Durusha, the King of Kadesh. It is notable for being the first battle in history for which there are detailed accounts. These were created by the scribe Tjaneni and carved into hieroglyphs in the Halls of Annals at the Temple of Amun. The Egyptians were victorious.

The Battle of Kadesh (below), fought in what is now Syria, took place in 1275 B.C. It is the earliest known battle in which true military tactics were used. The Hittite king, Muwatalli, ambushed the Egyptian army of

Ramses II, which included 1,500 chariots. However, the Egyptians claimed that they emerged the victors.

A resulting treaty was the first superpower peace treaty in history and can been seen inscribed on temple walls in Luxor, Egypt (right), while the original tablet is on display at the Istanbul Archaeological Museum.

"*I charged all countries*"

Ramses II at the Battle of Kadesh, 1275 B.C.

FACT FILE

The bloodiest battle in history?

The greatest proportionate loss of life in a military disaster occurred in 255 B.C., during the First Punic War. A Roman fleet of 364 ships, that had just inflicted a crushing defeat on the Carthaginians (200 ships) off Cape Hermaeum, was wrecked in a storm off Camarina, Sicily, with the loss of all but 80 vessels and perhaps 100,000 men, estimated as around 15 percent of the adult male population of Italy. The Romans managed to rebuild their fleet and train new crews to continue the war against Carthage.

INFLATED NUMBERS

The further back in time you go, the more unreliable battlefield statistics become.

Ancient and medieval writers in particular were notorious for exaggerating the size of armies. There were several reasons for this. First, it was extremely difficult to collate accurate figures regarding the size of each side's army and casualty figures,

especially as writers were often receiving statistics second-hand from unreliable sources. Second, for the victorious side, exaggerating enemy numbers made the triumph all the more spectacular. Third, and conversely, defeats could be better explained if the enemy had overwhelming numbers.

THERMOPYLAE

The Battle of Thermopylae (below) took place in 480 B.C. between around 4,000 Greeks (including the famous 300 Spartans) and 100,000 Persians. Ancient writers told a different story. According to Herodotus, some 5,283,220 Persians were at Thermopylae. The poet Simonides, who was a near-contemporary, talks of four million. Ctesias of Cnidus, Artaxerxes Mnemon's personal physician, wrote a history of Persia using Persian sources. He gives 800,000 as the total number of the Persian Army that met in Doriskos, Thrace, after crossing the Hellespont.

The Persians won the battle, but went on to lose the war.

THE MONGOL HORDES

The Mongol horsemen of Genghis Khan struck terror into their foes during the thirteenth century. Though undoubtedly cruel, the numbers of their victims were wildly exaggerated by medieval writers. Describing the capture of Baghdad in 1258, the writer

FACT FILE

- -

Some very unequal battles in history

• Battle of Plassey (June 23, 1757): Robert Clive (3,000 British troops and sepoys) defeats Siraj-ud-Daula (52,000 ill-trained levies) with the help of a thunderstorm and highly disciplined Redcoats.

• Battle of Rorke's Drift (January 22, 1879): 139 British troops armed with Martini Henry breech-loading rifles defeat 4,500 Zulus.

• Operation Desert Storm (February 1991): Iraqi dictator Saddam Hussein kindly lines up his 500,000 troops in the desert so that the United Nations' Coalition force can outflank and destroy them, after first subjecting them to weeks of aerial bombardment.

• Operation Iraqi Freedom (April–May 2003): A U.S.-led army of 300,000 destroys Saddam Hussein's one million troops in six weeks.

Al-Maqrizi reported that the Mongols killed two million people.

A Franciscan friar, who in 1245 went to seek out the Great Khan in the hope of persuading him to become a Christian (some hope), reported that, during a siege of a Chinese city, a Mongol army ran out of food and ate one of every 10 of its own soldiers. Actually, Mongol armies (above) were often outnumbered on the battlefield.

In Hungary and Poland, for example, the Mongols were outnumbered but tactically superior to their opponents.

BATTLE CASUALTIES

Battles are bloody affairs, but sometimes a combination of factors can produce bizarre results, where one side suffers hardly any casualties, while the other is decimated.

FACT FILE

Lopsided battle casualties

• Battle of Anchialus (August 20, 917): Some 110,000 Byzantine troops under Leo Phocas were crushed by 70,000 Bulgarians led by Simeon the Great. Byzantine losses were allegedly 70,000 killed.

• Battle of Lepanto (October 7, 1571): An Ottoman fleet (285 ships) under Ali Pasha was defeated by a Holy League fleet (212 ships) under Don John of Austria (shown above). The Ottoman Turks lost 210 ships, the Holy League a mere 50.

• Battle of Zenta (September 11, 1697): 30,000 Hapsburg troops under Prince Eugene of Savoy lost 428 of their number, while inflicting over 30,000 casualties on the 100,000-strong Turkish army under Sultan Mustafa II.

Oddballs

On November 18, 1822, the *London Observer* reported that the Napoleonic battlefields of Leipzig, Austerlitz, and Waterloo had been harvested of all their human and horse bones, which had been shipped to Yorkshire, England, to be turned into fertilizer. Who says recycling is a new thing?

MILITARY MADNESS

The Charge of the Light Brigade (below)

The charge of the British Light Brigade at the Battle of Balaclava on October 25, 1854, during the Crimean War, showed the folly of attacking artillery head on. Out of 673 cavalrymen who took part, 195 returned with their mounts, 113 were killed, and the rest returned to their own lines on foot. Of the survivors, 247 were wounded.

MILITARY MADNESS

The problem with laying millions of mines is that when hostilities end, it's too much of an effort to dig them up. In World War II, both the Allies and Axis took to planting mines in Egypt with gusto, with the result that there are today an estimated 23 million still lying in the ground over an area of 10 million square miles (26 million square km). And the mines deny access to a landmass of approximately 22 percent of Egypt's territory. To date, more than 8,000 Egyptians

have been injured or killed by German, Italian, and British mines since the end of World War II.

"Constantly strive for maximum performance"

Field Marshal Erwin Rommel, North Africa, 1942

NON-BATTLE CASUALTIES

Not all soldiers die in battle; indeed, more have often died away from the field of honor.

THE ROYAL NAVY
Of the estimated 100,000 Royal Navy personnel who died in the service between 1793 and 1815, during a period of protracted war with France, as well as the War of 1812 with the United States, plus a number of smaller campaigns around the world, only around seven percent died in combat. Some 80 percent died of disease or in accidents, and 13 percent were drowned at sea.

WORLD WAR II
During World War II, the Soviet Union suffered a daily average death rate of 19,014 men, women, and children. When the Germans retreated from the Ukraine in late 1943 and early 1944, for example, they conducted a scorched earth policy to deny supplies and shelter to the advancing Red Army. In the process, they destroyed more than 28,000 villages and 714 cities and towns, leaving 10,000,000 people without shelter. They also wiped out 16,000 industrial enterprises, more than 200,000 industrial production sites, 27,910 collective and 872 state farms, and 1300 machine and tractor stations. By the end of the war, around

35 million Soviets, both military and civilian, were dead.

BATTLEFIELD MEDICINE
Battlefield medicine (above) was a great killer up to the beginning of the twentieth century. It wasn't until the mid-sixteenth century, for example, that a French Army surgeon named Ambroise Paré discovered that amputees had a better chance of survival if he avoided cauterization in favor of tying off the exposed blood vessels.

HAILSTORM OF LEAD

Modern artillery systems can unleash a storm of steel.

VERDUN

At the Battle of Verdun (February–October 1916), approximately 1,700 French artillery pieces (below) fired 23 million rounds, more than 13,500 rounds per gun.

EL ALAMEIN

The British fired 530,000 rounds in 24 hours, an average of 22,083.3 per hour, from the 1,030 guns and howitzers during their opening barrage at the Battle of El Alamein on October 23, 1942.

PATTON'S BOYS

During the U.S. Third Army's advance across Europe (August 1, 1944, through 8 May 1945), artillery units of the army fired an average of 20,892.7 rounds per day.

Oddballs

When the ammunition runs out, use rocks.
During the American Civil War, at the Battle of Manassas (August 29–30, 1862), one Confederate unit ran out of ammunition and had to throw rocks at the oncoming Federals. Curiously, instead of firing their small arms, some Union troops responded in kind and began hurling rocks back. Similarly, during the fighting for Monte Nero on the Austro-Italian Front, on June 2, 1915, when the troops ran out of ammunition they also took to throwing rocks at each other.

FACT FILE

World War I killing grounds

Battle	Date	Casualties
First Champagne (Germans vs French)	December 20, 1914–March 17, 1915	90,000 Germans, 95,000 French
Loos (below) (Germans vs British)	September 25–October 19, 1915	25,000 Germans, 50,000 British
Second Champagne (Germans vs French)	September 25–November 6, 1915	85,000 Germans, 143,500 French
Verdun (Germans vs French)	February 21–December 18, 1916	434,000 Germans, 550,000 French
Somme (Germans vs British and French)	July 1–November 18, 1916	680,000 Germans, 419,600 British, 204,000 French
Arras (Germans vs British)	April 9–May 16, 1917	120,000 Germans, 160,000 British
Second Aisne (Germans vs French)	April 16–May 9, 1917	168,000 Germans, 187,000 French
Passchendaele (Germans vs British)	July 31–November 10, 1917	260,000 Germans, 310,000 British
Operation Michael (Germans vs British and French)	March 21–April 5, 1918	348,000 Germans, 236,000 British, 92,000 French

FACT FILE

Vietnam War myths

Myth: The common belief is that the fighting in Vietnam was not as intense as in World War II.

Fact: The average infantryman in the South Pacific during World War II saw about 40 days of combat in four years. The average infantryman in Vietnam (below) saw about 240 days of combat in one year. One out of every 10 Americans who served in Vietnam was a casualty—58,148 were killed and 304,000 wounded out of 2.7 million who served.

Myth: Drug use was rampant among American troops in Vietnam.

Fact: The overwhelming percentage of American drug users in the 1960s were in fact civilians, and a very high percentage of antiwar activists were drug users.

Myth: American atrocities were widespread during the war.

Fact: Only two documented cases of war crimes can be attributed to U.S. military personnel—the slaughter of civilians in March 1968 at the village of My Lai, and the murder of 16 women and children at Son Thang-4 on February 19, 1970.

BATTLEFIELD MYTHS

Sometimes the truth gets buried along with the losing side's dead.

THE MYTH OF SPARTAN INVINCIBILITY

They didn't win every battle. Caught in a narrow defile between some steep hills and a swamp near Tegyra in 375 B.C., a small Theban army under Pelopides (no more than the 300 hoplites of the "Sacred Band" plus a handful of cavalrymen) was ambushed by five times its number of Spartans.

Some of the Theban troops panicked. Remaining calm, Pelopides led his men right into the center of the Spartan force, which promptly broke and ran away.

THE CRASSUS MYTH

Killed by the Parthians after the Battle of Carrhae in 53 B.C., the Roman general Marcus Licinius Crassus was decapitated and his head subjected to many insults. However, it is a myth that molten gold was poured down the head's throat.

THE MYTH OF THE BAYONET IN BATTLE

Bayonet attacks (above) are actually rare. For example, of 240,000 wounds treated by Union medical officers during the American Civil War, fewer than 1,000 had been inflicted by the bayonet.

THE MYTH OF THE TAXIS THAT SAVED PARIS

The famed "Taxis of the Marne," which so gallantly conveyed thousands of reinforcements from Paris to the front in the critical early days of World War I, quite patriotically had their meters running for the entire trip.

TANKS IN BATTLE

Steel monsters crushing all in their path is the popular image of tanks. This isn't always the case, though.

HUSSITE TANKS

Early tanks were in fact made of wood, not metal. During the Hussite Wars (1420–34), the Hussite commander, Jan Zizka (right), developed the War Wagon—a sturdy, four-wheeled peasant cart made of strong wood (with a crew of 18). The success of the War Wagon strategy led to various improvements in their design, notably an armored exterior with gun notches, movable boards to protect the wheels, and a stabilizing spike that would anchor the wagon in place. In battle, the wagons were arranged in a circular formation, linked together with heavy chains, with extremely large shield bearers between the gaps in the wagons.

MECHANICAL BREAKDOWN

In World War II, many tanks broke down before they got to grips with the enemy. The fearsome German Tiger I tank (below) was prone to mechanical breakdowns, and needed constant repairs and maintenance to keep it operational. At one point it was forbidden to run the Tiger tank for long periods to prevent overtaxing the drivetrains. Ultimately, more Tiger Is were lost due to mechanical breakdown than were lost to enemy action. And more German Jagdtiger tank destroyers were lost to mechanical problems or lack of fuel than to enemy action. Enemy action accounted for only 25 percent of the tanks lost by the British Army in France in 1940; all the rest were due to mechanical breakdown.

"The tank is the weapon of decisive attack"

General Heinz Guderian, 1937

MILITARY MADNESS

The quest for size

During World War II, tank designers became obsessed by size, and began developing bigger and bigger tanks. The result was a complete waste of resources.

TANK NAME	WEIGHT	MAIN ARMAMENT	COUNTRY	FATE
Heavy Tank M6	126,000 lb (57,500 kg)	3in gun	USA	project scrapped in December 1944
A39	174,720 lb (79,250 kg)	94mm gun	UK	war ended before production started
Maus	422,400 lb (192,000 kg)	128mm gun	Germany	war ended before production started

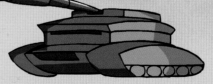

GENERALS, HEROES, AND VILLAINS

War produces its fair share of the great, the brave, the bad, and, er, the short.

SHORT COMMANDERS: SIZE ISN'T EVERYTHING

Field Marshal the Viscount Bernard Law Montgomery of El Alamein fame wore "elevator" boots and shoes, with special inserts so that he could appear taller.

The shortest American general possibly ever was Brigadier General John H. "Pee Wee" Collier, commander of Combat Command A, 2nd Armored Division, in northwest Europe, 1944–45. He was just 5 ft 2 in (1.57 m) tall.

"Tom Thumb" was the nickname of British Vice Admiral Tom Phillips, who commanded the *Prince of Wales* and *Repulse* when they were sunk by Japanese aircraft on December 10, 1941. He went down with his ship, the *Prince of Wales*. He was just 5 ft 4 in (1.62 m) tall.

But what about Napoleon (below)? Because the old French inch was about eight percent longer than the English inch, Napoleon, at 5ft 2in (1.57 m) French style, has been thought of as being short. Actually he was 5 ft 6 in (1.67 m)—average for his time.

YOUNG GUNS

History's youngest generals:

ALEXANDER THE GREAT
(356–323 B.C.) Macedon, 16 (right)

CHARLES XII (1682–1718)
Sweden, 18

EDWARD, THE BLACK PRINCE
(1330–76) England, 17

GUSTAVUS ADOLPHUS
(1594–1632) Sweden, 17

HENRI IV (1553–1610)
France, 16

JEANNE D'ARC (1412–31)
France, 17

WILLIAM I (1027–87)
Normandy, 19

However, they take second place to King Jaime I of Aragon (1213–76), later called "the Conqueror." Having inherited the throne of an unruly kingdom on the death of his older brother, he took the field against rebellious barons, an undertaking in which, with the help of some able advisors, he was successful, despite being only 11 at the time.

MILITARY MADNESS

Invited by his great uncle, Julius Caesar, to serve on campaign with him in Spain in 45 B.C., 18-year old Gaius Octavius, later the Emperor Augustus, put together a small party of friends to accompany him. He had to reject one volunteer who wanted to tag along, though—his mother, Atia.

MILITARY MADNESS

Insanity doesn't necessarily inhibit military success, but it can be very tiresome for allies. Marshal Blücher (left), the Prussian commander who saved the day at Waterloo in 1815, was as mad as a hatter. At one time he told the Duke of Wellington that he was pregnant with an elephant that had been sired by a French soldier, while at other times he jumped around his room or walked on tip-toes, believing that the French had increased the underfloor heating to intolerable levels.

GOLDEN OLDIES

Great age does not necessarily prohibit battlefield command.

In 1204, the Venetian Doge Enrico Dandolo directed the siege and capture of Constantinople by the Fourth Crusade. He was 97 at the time and also blind.

General Winfield Scott (1786–1866), right, was the Union commander-in-chief at the start of the Civil War in 1861, when he was 75 years old. Not far behind was Confederate General David Emanuel Twiggs (1790–1862), who was 71 years old in 1861.

FACT FILE

One-eyed commanders

• Hannibal (247–183 B.C.), the great Carthaginian commander, lost an eye to an infection during his campaign in Italy.

• King Philip II of Macedon (359–36 B.C.), the father of Alexander the Great, lost an eye in battle.

• Andre Massena (1758–1817), one of Napoleon's marshals, was accidentally blinded in one eye in 1808 by Marshal Berthier during a shooting party. Bad luck.

• Lord Nelson (1758–1805), right, lost the sight of his right eye in action in 1794.

• Sir Archibald Wavell (1883–1950), who commanded in Southeast Asia, the Middle East, and later India during World War II, lost an eye in 1915 in Flanders.

• Moshe Dayan (1915–81), the Israeli general and later defense minister, lost an eye on campaign against the Vichy French in Syria in 1941.

At present, the most "famous" one-eyed commander is Mullah Omar of the Taliban.

MASTERS OF WAR

HELMUTH VON MOLTKE (1800–91), the genius reformer of the Prussian Army and the creator of its General Staff (below), directed the Prussian victories over Austria in 1866 and over France in 1870–71. He was literate in several languages, including English, Latin, Italian, French, and Greek, and kept a diary in three languages interchangeably: English, Italian, and French. Moltke was also an author of some note, producing numerous short stories, novels, historical essays, and other works of considerable literary merit. Curiously, despite his enormous experience, including a tour of duty as an advisor to the Turkish Army during the 1840s, until 1866, when he held supreme command under the Kaiser, he had never directed even a small body of troops in battle.

"Great achievements, small display"

Helmuth von Moltke,
on the Prussian General Staff

THE OTHER ROMMEL
Erwin Rommel is well known as the "Desert Fox." But there was another General Rommel in World War II: Lieutenant General Juliusz Rommel of the Polish Army. He endured nearly six years (1939–45) in a German prisoner-of-war camp, and was one of over 5,000 Polish prisoners liberated when American troops overran a large prison camp at Murnau. After the war, he lived in retirement, dying in 1967 at well over 80 years of age.

LITTLE TURTLE

Little Turtle (1747–1812), right, was one of the greatest of all Native American war leaders, and was raised in Ohio. In the late summer of 1790, Brigadier General Josiah Harmer was sent into Ohio with 320 regulars and 1,100 militia to put down Indian insurrectionists. The latter's hit-and-run tactics soon forced Harmer to retreat, having lost 183 men killed and many wounded.

On the evening of November 3, U.S. troops were 100 miles (160 km) north of Cincinnati, at Kekionga. Little Turtle attacked the ill-guarded camp at dawn the next day. The result was 637 U.S. soldiers killed and 263 wounded. It was one of the most crushing defeats in American military history.

Oddballs

Some of America's greatest generals and admirals have been of German descent, including John J. Pershing (World War I); Henry Arnold (World War II), the chief of the Army Air Forces; Dwight D. Eisenhower (World War II); Carl Spaatz (World War II), who was responsible for bombing Germany; Walter Krueger (World War II, actually born in Germany); Robert L. Eichelberger (World War II); Albert C. Wedemeyer (World War II); Chester W. Nimitz (World War II); Marc Mitscher (World War II); Harry Schmidt (World War II); and Norman Schwarzkopf (Persian Gulf War).

RUTHLESS LEADERS

RICHARD III
On the eve of the Battle of Bosworth (August 22, 1485), King Richard III of England found a sentry asleep at his post and promptly killed him with his dagger.

HENRY V
Up to 12,000 people starved to death between the lines during Henry V's siege of Rouen, France, in 1418–19. The garrison had driven all the "useless mouths" out of the town. Henry (left) refused to let them escape.

SIR JOHN HAWKWOOD
In 1370, this mercenary came across two of his men arguing over who should rape a young nun they had captured. He solved the problem by stabbing her to death.

MILITARY MADNESS

Killing your own officers is one way, albeit extreme, of resolving command disputes. At the Battle of Tewkesbury (May 4, 1471), the Duke of Somerset relieved Lord Wenlock, who fought for both Yorkists and Lancastrians during the Wars of the Roses, for moving his forces so slowly that the battle was lost. His method of relief was to take an axe and split open Wenlock's skull. Painful!

MEN OF HONOR

War does not have to mean
an absence of civility.

RICHARD THE LIONHEART AND SALADIN

During the Third Crusade in the twelfth century, the two protagonists, King Richard of England (1157–99) and Saladin, Sultan of Egypt (1137–93), maintained a cordial relationship. When Richard's horse was slain during a battle, for example, Saladin sent him two new mounts, with the message: "A gift from one king to another." On another occasion, learning that Richard was ill, Saladin (who was an amateur physician) sent his foe a daily basket of fresh fruit. Richard, in turn, sent Saladin two prize falcons, so that the sultan could indulge his passion for hunting.

GEORGE WASHINGTON

On October 4, 1777, George Washington (right) attacked Sir William Howe's army at Germantown. His plan failed, but Washington's troops captured Sir William's dog. Being a gentleman, on October 6, Washington wrote to his adversary: "General Washington's compliments to General Howe. He does himself the pleasure to return to him a dog, which accidentally fell into his hands, and by the inscription on the collar appears to belong to General Howe."

"FIGHTING BOB" EVANS

After Spanish sailors had struggled ashore following the destruction of the Spanish squadron at Santiago on July 3, 1898, some were murdered by Cuban troops. Captain Robley "Fighting Bob" Evans, of the battleship *Iowa,* was so incensed by this that he sent a detail of U.S. Marines ashore to protect the helpless men. He informed the local Cubans that if they did not "cease this infamous work" he would turn his guns on them. It did the trick—they stopped their murderous actions.

STRANGE DEATHS

Not all generals are killed in battle, though some must have wished that they had been.

The Roman Emperor Carinus (250–285) was killed at the Battle of the Margus Valley in 285. Not by the enemy, but by one of his own officers whose wife he had seduced.

After losing to a Byzantine army in 626, the Persian general Shahin was executed by his sovereign, Shah Khushrau II, by being first skinned alive and then salted down.

The Russian people can be a fiery lot. So it's perhaps no surprise to learn that in 1610 they stormed the Kremlin in Moscow to depose the "False" Dimitry II. They then tortured the usurper, killed him, burned his body, and fired the ashes out of a cannon toward Poland, his chief supporter.

LUCKY GENERALS

MARSHAL OUDINOT

Despite the fact that between 1793 and 1814 Napoleon's Marshal Oudinot (1767–1847) was wounded an average of 1.4 times per year, accumulating a total of 24 wounds, he died peacefully in his bed in 1847 at the age of 80.

GENERAL FORREST

In the American Civil War, the Confederate cavalry leader, Nathan Bedford Forrest (1821–77), left, suffered four major wounds and had 29 horses shot from under him, but survived the conflict.

Oddballs

MILITARY MADNESS

Marshal Ney (1769–1815), right, was called the "bravest of the brave" by Napoleon. During his career he was wounded at the siege of Mainz (1794), at Winterthur (1799), at Smolensk (1812), and at Leipzig (1813). At the Battle of Waterloo (1815) he had four horses shot from under him. Despite his best efforts to get himself killed during the battle, he failed. He was actually shot by a French royalist firing squad following the return of King Louis XVIII (1755–1824). Ney refused to wear a blindfold and said to the firing squad: "Soldiers, aim straight for the heart!"

THE HITLER CONNECTION

In September 1918, on the French battlefield of Marcoing, in the last weeks of World War I, English "Tommy" Private Henry Tandey, who served with the Duke of Wellington's Regiment, won the Victoria Cross for bravery. The 27 year old knocked out a machine-gun nest and also led a bayonet charge. As the Battle of Marcoing raged, Allied and German forces engaged in bitter hand-to-hand combat. The defining moment for Private Tandey and world history came when a wounded German limped directly into his line of fire on September 28, 1918:

"I took aim, but couldn't shoot a wounded man," said Tandey, "so I let him go." The young German soldier nodded in gratitude and retreated with the rest of the German Army. Years later, Tandey discovered he had spared an Austrian corporal named Adolf Hitler (above).

Oddballs

William Patrick Hitler was the nephew of Adolf Hitler (1889–1945), being the son of Hitler's half-brother, Alois Jr. He served in the U.S. Navy in World War II. Curiously, when he enlisted on March 6, 1944, the recruiting officer who signed him up was a man named Hess. Heinrich "Heinz" Hitler, another nephew of the *Führer*, served as a 19-year-old noncommissioned signals officer in the German 23rd Artillery Regiment during Operation Barbarossa, the German 1941 invasion of the Soviet Union. He was captured in January 1942 and disappeared into the Soviet prison camp system, where he was murdered.

On becoming German chancellor in 1933, Hitler (left) ordered his staff to track down Tandey's service records. They also obtained a print of an Italian painting showing Tandey carrying a wounded Allied soldier on his back, which Hitler hung with pride on the wall at his mountain-top retreat at Berchtesgaden.

Years later, Tandey remarked: "If only I had known what he would turn out to be. When I saw all the people, women and children, he had killed and wounded I was sorry to God I let him go." Tandey died in 1977 at the age of 86.

FACT FILE

Mein Kampf

Hitler's autobiographical work, *Mein Kampf* (*My Struggle*), is a turgid piece of writing, full of rambling, inane passages. Despite the fact that 10 million copies had been sold by 1945, most were never read. Even die-hard Nazis rarely had the stamina to wade through it all, most giving up in the early chapters.

HEROES ON AND OFF THE SILVER SCREEN

During World War II, Donald Pleasance (1919–95), later a famous Hollywood actor, served in the British Royal Air Force until he was shot down and captured. He was sent to the infamous Stalag Luft III, where he played an important role in planning the famous "Great Escape," for which he received a "Mention in Dispatches" from the British Air Ministry. He later went on to act in the 1963 Hollywood film about the escape attempt.

"It doesn't bother me much that I'm probably hopelessly typecast"

Donald Pleasance

The British actor Richard Todd (1919–2009), left, a captain in the 7th Battalion, Parachute Regiment, jumped into Normandy on D-Day (June 6, 1944), and was among the first troops to reach Pegasus Bridge at Bénouville. The bridge had earlier been captured by an advanced party from the 2nd Battalion, Oxfordshire and Buckinghamshire Light Infantry, commanded by Major John Howard. Todd later portrayed Howard in the film *The Longest Day*, in which an unaccredited actor played Todd.

KINGS IN BATTLE

Richard III (1452–85) was the last reigning English monarch to be killed in battle, at Bosworth in 1485. The last English king to command troops on the battlefield was George II (right). In 1743, aged 60, his men defeated the French at the Battle of Dettingen.

The last occasion on which kings commanded on both sides in a battle was at the Slivnitsa, November 5–7, 1885, when the Serbians under King Milan were soundly beaten by the Bulgarians under Prince Alexander Battenberg.

MILITARY MADNESS

At the Battle of Königgrätz (July 3, 1866), King Wilhelm I of Prussia (1797–1888), left, interfered so often in the conduct of operations that Chancellor Otto von Bismarck (1815–98), present as an observer, reportedly gave the royal steed a swift kick in the rump, causing it to panic and run from the field. This removed the king from the scene long enough for the army commander, Helmuth von Moltke, to win the battle against the Austrians.

EMBEZZLERS

The most adept embezzler in military history was almost certainly Tomas Lopez de Ulloa, the paymaster of the Spanish Army of Flanders from 1642 to 1651. He was so capable at fraud that it required 50 years of meticulous investigation and auditing before the Spanish government was able to determine that his estate owed the Crown 309,325 florins, enough money to pay 30,000 soldiers for one day.

In the modern age, a retired Israeli general, Alex Eyal, embezzled an estimated $10 million of U.S. foreign military aid. In 1991, retired Israeli general Rami Dotan was indicted for embezzling some $40 million in U.S. foreign military aid with the assistance of Herbert Steindler, an official of the American Pratt & Whitney aircraft engine manufacturer. Dotan was imprisoned for his actions.

TRUE GRIT

Audie Murphy (opposite page) was a true American hero and the most decorated U.S. soldier of World War II. Murphy portrayed himself (Gordon Gebert played Murphy as a boy) in the 1955 movie *To Hell and Back*, which was based on the book of the same name, Murphy's autobiography.

Oddballs

When America was struck on September 11, 2001, President George W. Bush was widely criticized in the liberal press for waiting seven minutes before reacting to the news of the terrorist attacks. However, Franklin D. Roosevelt waited 22 minutes before reacting to the news of the bombing of Pearl Harbor in 1941.

FACT FILE

- -

Audie Murphy's awards

- Medal of Honor
- Distinguished Service Cross
- Silver Star with First Oak Leaf Cluster
- Bronze Star Medal with "V" Device and First Oak Leaf Cluster
- Purple Heart with Second Oak Leaf Cluster
- Distinguished Unit Emblem with First Oak Leaf Cluster
- Campaign Medal with one silver service star, three bronze service stars, and one bronze service arrowhead
- French *Croix de Guerre* with silver star
- Belgian *Croix de Guerre* 1940 with PalmGood Conduct Medal
- American Campaign Medal
- European-African-Middle Eastern World War II Victory Medal
- Combat Infantry Badge
- Marksman Badge with Rifle Bar
- Expert Badge with Bayonet Bar
- French *Fourragère* in colors of the *Croix de Guerre*
- French Legion of Honor, Grade of *Chevalier*
- Legion of Merit

FIGHTING FOR BOTH SIDES

Changing sides is risky in war, though some have managed it remarkably effortlessly. In the spring of 1775, for example, Ezekiel Polk, a young man from a landed family, joined the North Carolina militia to do his bit for the American Revolution. On June 17, his comrades elected him captain of their company. However, within two months Polk and his entire company deserted to the British side.

Then, little more than two months later, in November, they all deserted back to the American side!

Surprisingly, despite this display of a certain degree of treachery, Polk was allowed to retain his command. In fact, by the end of the Revolutionary War he had risen to the rank of lieutenant colonel of militia and regimental commander.

HEDGING YOUR BETS

Far less risky is having family members on both sides. Here are a few examples from the American Civil War.

Brothers Frederick Hubbard, a Confederate, and Henry Hubbard, a Union supporter, met each other at the Battle of Bull Run, being placed side by side in hospital after being wounded.

"Jeb" Stuart's chief of staff, Major H.B. McClellan, had four brothers who fought for the Union, plus a first cousin, George McClellan (commander of the Army of the Potomac).

Confederate General Patrick Cleburne had one brother fighting for the Southern cause and another brother in the Union Army.

Captain John L. Inglis, an Englishman fighting for the Confederacy, captured a battery of Union guns commanded by his brother.

MILITARY MADNESS

In 1639, during the First Bishop's War in Scotland (right), discovering that her son, the Marquis of Hamilton (below), was preparing to land a royalist army on the shores of the Firth of Forth, Lady Anne Cunningham, a staunch opponent of King Charles I of England, organized a troop of horse and rode out to oppose him, keeping a special pistol ready and loaded, should she encounter her son. The meeting never took place, but the marquis came to a bad end, being found guilty of treason and beheaded at Westminster on March 9, 1649.

FAKES AND CHARLATANS

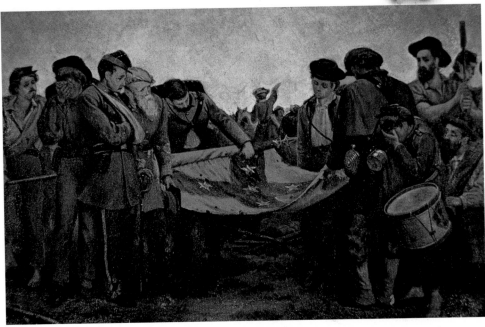

WALTER WILLIAMS

Williams, of Houston, Texas, who died in 1959, is widely believed to have been the last surviving Confederate soldier. He was given a lavish funeral. Around 100,000 people watched his funeral procession through the heart of Houston, the hearse escorted by reenactors in Confederate gray. Williams was buried with full military honors, including a firing party in Confederate gray, with widespread national press and television coverage. However, Williams was not a veteran. Born in 1855, he never served a day in the Confederate Army (above). As he grew older, he began pretending to have served in the Civil War, retelling tales of the war that he had heard as a child from real veterans. In 1932, in the depths of the Depression, he applied for the pension that Texas granted to all Confederate veterans. With his neighbors—who had been listening to his war stories for years—testifying as to his status, the pension was quickly granted. In 1936, Congress extended full veterans' status to the handful of surviving Confederate vets, including Walter Williams.

REX CRANE

Crane was a celebrated war hero who rose to become head of the Prisoner of War Association of Australia. Turns out, though, Crane didn't serve in World War II and never saw the inside of a Japanese prison camp. Indeed, what he knew about fighting in the jungles of Malaya or the brutality of Japanese jail guards (left) he had gleaned from books. Worse, he had never enlisted and had never worn a uniform.

Oddballs

Spare a thought for the Roman general Scipio Aemilianus, who commanded the army that besieged, captured, and then destroyed the city of Carthage in 146 B.C. It all got too much for him and he broke down in tears as his men burned the city.

BATTLEFIELD BLUNDERS

Disaster is never far away, especially if your army is led by the arrogant, incompetent, and stupid.

AWFUL ARMIES

Men serving in the Austrian Army (below) must be ranked among the unluckiest in history. In 1788, the Austrian emperor, Joseph II (1741–90), went to war against the Turks in Transylvania. After camping in some marshland, 172,000 of his troops caught malaria, of whom 33,000 died.

Undeterred, Joseph took half his army to meet the Turks near the town of Karansebes. On the way, some infantrymen bought some local brew from some peasants, whereupon their officers reprimanded them. The men took offense, and, in order to frighten the officers away, started shouting out that the Turks were upon them. The officers believed them and raised the false alarm. Panic spread throughout the army and a stampede ensued. Austrians started fighting Austrians and many men were also drowned in the river or were crushed. By daybreak, it became apparent that the Austrians had killed 10,000 of their own number. The Turks had still not even arrived!

On the eve of the Italian War of 1859, despite the fact that 68 percent (255,000) of the 375,000 Austrian reservists mobilized were so ill trained that they couldn't load a musket, Austria decided to go to war anyway, with disastrous consequences (defeat and 16,000 dead).

In the aftermath of their disastrous war with Japan in 1894–95 (First Sino-Japanese War), the Chinese, who had discovered that their rifles did not work very well with the substandard rounds with which they were supplied, decided to scrap the guns rather than acquire new ammunition.

Oddballs

The Italian Army of World War II, often the butt of jokes concerning its cowardice, was, in fact, a decent fighting force, let down by poor equipment and bad leadership. In North Africa, for example, the Italians supplied the bulk of Axis troops, and many German victories, such as at Gazala in 1942, were the result of Italian skill-at-arms and a combined Axis effort. As a final word, the British Gurkhas, who encountered Italian troops (right) in Greece in 1941, rated them as tough soldiers, and *they* should know.

INCOMPETENCE

There has never been a shortage of incompetent officers to ensure defeat.

THE BATTLE OF BANNOCKBURN

At Bannockburn on June 24, 1314 (right), Edward II positioned his army so that it could barely maneuver, while he kept his bowmen at the rear, rendering them useless. Worst of all, he left the battle while the issue was in the balance; his troops saw this and fled, handing victory to Robert the Bruce. It was the most disastrous English defeat since the Battle of Hastings in 1066.

THE SIEGE OF BEAUVAIS

In 1472, the Lord of Cordes brought two cannon to lay siege to the French town of Beauvais. Unfortunately, he brought only *two* cannon balls, which, although they did excellent work, proved insufficient to breach the walls.

EXPEDITION TO CADIZ

After capturing Fort Puntal from the Spanish during the November 1625 expedition to Cadiz, the leader of the English troops, Sir Edward Cecil, ordered his men to camp in a field next to some deserted buildings, which housed gallons and gallons of wine. Within less than an hour his troops were drunk, with fights breaking out, men shooting at each other, and others threatening any officer who tried to maintain discipline. The next morning the hungover army discarded its equipment and headed for home (the 100 men who had stayed behind to sleep off their hangovers were all killed by the Spanish).

"There is always hazard in military movements"

General Robert E. Lee, June 8, 1863

THE BATTLE OF THE SOMME

World War I was a breeding ground for incompetence. The 1916 Battle of the Somme was a case in point. After a week-long artillery bombardment to destroy the German defenses and to cut the forests of barbed wire, the British troops attacked on July 1. They were told that they would meet "nothing but dead and wounded Germans." The King's Own Yorkshire Light Infantry were even told to light their pipes and cigarettes, as they would meet no live Germans. But the Germans were very much alive and were waiting with machine guns. The result was 20,000 British dead on the first day alone.

MILITARY MADNESS

After the Battle of Gettysburg (July 1–3, 1863), the Army of Northern Virginia was a spent force. General Lee was gathering his badly mauled forces and trying to get back to Virginia. In his way was the rain-swollen Potomac River. It was the perfect opportunity for the Army of the Potomac, which had several reserves that had seen little if any fighting, to deliver the final blow. All that remained was for General Meade (right) to give the order to attack. The order never came. Instead, Meade waited (no one knows for what). President Lincoln was incensed. The result was General Grant being called east from Vicksburg to take up command of the Army of the Potomac. But the Civil War would drag on for two more bloody years.

ARROGANCE

Being confident is one thing, but being arrogant can lead to disaster.

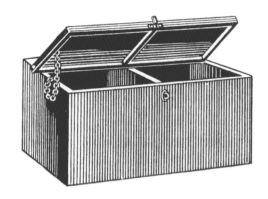

ADMIRAL CLOWDESLEY SHOVELL

On the night of October 22, 1707, Admiral Sir Clowdesley Shovell made a navigational error that led to the loss of four British warships and more than 1,300 lives, including his own, on the rocks off the Scilly Isles. Just a few hours before, he had hanged a seaman as a mutineer for telling him that the squadron was off course.

CHARLES BRANDON

The 1824 Ashanti War was an example of supreme incompetence by Charles Brandon, the British military stores manager.

The British soldiers, having been surrounded by 10,000 Ashanti warriors, were running low on ammunition and looked to Brandon to break open the reserve rounds. As the Ashanti warriors closed in, Brandon unscrewed the ammunition boxes, only to find that they were full of biscuits. He had brought the wrong supplies.

GENERAL SIR GEORGE COLLEY

Another British disaster took place at the Battle of Majuba Hill (left). In January 1881, General Sir George Colley decided to invade the Transvaal, South Africa. After suffering an initial defeat, he reckoned that attacking the Boers from the 6000 ft (1829 m) Majuba Hill would give him a much needed victory. Instead of digging in at the summit, the British started jeering at the Boer soldiers at the foot of the hill.

Oddballs

In 1898, during a period of rising tensions between the British Empire and the Boer Republic of South Africa, the British decided to impress upon the uncouth colonials the power and effectiveness of modern military technology. They therefore staged a demonstration of artillery fire. A flock of 100 sheep was driven onto a hill. A battery of the Royal Artillery then proceeded to shell the hill with gusto for 20 minutes. When the smoke cleared, it became apparent that all of the sheep were completely uninjured. Indeed, to add insult to injury, there were now in fact 101 sheep on the hill, for a pregnant ewe had delivered during the bombardment. The British attempt to intimidate the Boers into submission had failed miserably.

Colley decided to take a nap. Soon, a few hundred ragtag Boers (right) started climbing up the hill, while their comrades provided covering fire from below. Colley eventually awoke, launched a half-hearted counterattack, and was shot dead by a 12-year-old Boer; 93 other British soldiers were killed. The Boers lost one dead and five wounded.

UNDERESTIMATING THE ENEMY

Seeing the enemy as weak and a pushover is fine if they are indeed those things, but woe betide the general who dismisses the opposition too lightly.

In World War II, the British made the grave error of underestimating the Japanese. Before hostilities broke out, Japan's military capabilities were consistently undervalued. The most prevalent slur was the persistence of the belief that the Japanese as a race suffered from "slow mental adaptability." For example, Brigadier General C. R. Woodroffe observed

Oddballs

In the 1930s, the British believed that the Japanese could not be good pilots on account of them being carried on their mothers' backs when they were babies. This being the case, it was felt they had no sense of balance. In addition, British wisdom held that a further impediment to their flying prowess was that their limbs were too short to reach the controls in the cockpit. The British did not realize that the Japanese, building their own aircraft, would construct their cockpits to accommodate their own people.

Imperial Japanese Army annual maneuvers in 1919 and concluded, "to anyone familiar with the national psychology, it is doubtful whether the Japanese will ever become a first-class military soldier."

When the Japanese attacked in the Far East in 1941 (left), the British were in for a nasty shock. Yet even then, they underestimated their foes. The defenses of Hong Kong were breached because the British assumed that the Japanese did not wage night battles, and relaxed their guard accordingly during the hours of darkness.

SINGAPORE

The fall of Singapore to the Japanese in February 1942 was a great blow to British military prestige. Conventional British thinking held that Singapore was safe from a northern attack because the 500 miles (800 km) of dense jungle and rubber plantations of central Malaya were impassable by tanks. The British were wrong.

PEARL HARBOR

The Americans also underestimated the Japanese. On December 6, 1941, journalist Joseph Harsch asked whether the Japanese might try to bomb Pearl Harbor. Admiral Husband Kimmel (above, center), commanding the U.S. Pacific Fleet, replied, "I don't think they'd be such damned fools." The Japanese attacked the next day.

TOO MANY EQUALS DISASTER

The nineteenth-century Austro-Hungarian Army officially spoke no less than 10 languages. There were units that spoke German (25 percent of the army), Hungarian (23 percent), Czech (13 percent), Serbo-Croatian (9 percent), Polish (8 percent), Ukrainian (8 percent), Romanian (7 percent), Slovak (4 percent), Slovene (2 percent), and Italian (1 percent). All recruits had to learn about 800 words of "Command German," and all officers had to be fluent in both German and the language spoken in the regiment they were assigned to. It got worse when the reserves were called up, which increased the number of languages to 14.

During World War II, the Japanese Army had six different kinds of ammunition for its aircraft, while the Japanese Navy had seven, only one of which was interchangeable with that of the army.

SHORTSIGHTEDNESS

It seemed like a good idea
at the time.

THE BATTLE OF FONTENOY
At the Battle of Fontenoy on May 11,
1745 (opposite), the Anglo-Dutch-
Austrian Allies lost 40 of their 80
cannon because many of the guns were
served by civilian contractors, most of
whom decided to run away when they
realized that the battle was lost.

BOSTON (1775–76)
A shortage of cannon balls in the
Continental Army before Boston in
the winter of 1775–76 led an officer
to offer a cash reward for turning in
enemy balls. This led to a host of
broken ankles and occasional smashed
feet—George Washington ordered that
no one attempt to stop a cannonball
in motion.

THE BATTLE OF LÜTZEN
During the Battle of Lützen in
November 1632, Count Wallenstein,
the Imperial commander, mounted
"camp followers" on baggage horses
and mules to convince his enemy,
Gustavus Adolphus of Sweden, that he
had more cavalry than he did. The ruse
failed and Wallenstein lost the battle,
though Gustavus lost his life.

THE MAGINOT LINE
The great French defensive line was
not complete. Two major gaps existed:
one along the Belgian border
extending to the English Channel; and
the second across the wide swathe of
forested land in the Ardennes.
Considered too thick for tanks to pass
through, the Ardennes was the route
the German panzers took when they
invaded France in May 1940.

Oddballs

The Roman Empire was famed for its well-surfaced
roads, 180,000 miles (289,620 km) of them. Built as
straight as possible, they all led to Rome. This was
unfortunate in the later Roman Empire, as they actually
became a liability because invading barbarians could
travel along them just as quickly as Roman soldiers.

TOO OLD, TOO FAT

CHNODOMAR

Chnodomar, the German leader defeated by the Emperor Julian at Strasbourg in 357 (above), was so fat that when he fell off his horse he was unable to extract himself from the mud due to his own weight and that of his armor, and thus was captured by the Romans.

RUSSIAN GENERALS

Overweight commanders are also a modern phenomenon. In April 2008, so concerned was the Russian Defense Ministry about its portly generals that it launched a fitness regime to help them lose weight and squeeze into a new designer uniform. A third of the army's officers were overweight.

TOO OLD TO KEEP UP

So rapid was the Mameluke flight after being defeated by the Ottoman Turks under Selim the Grim at Marj Dabiq near Aleppo on August 24, 1516, that 80-year-old Sultan Ghowir of Syria was actually trampled to death by his own panic-stricken troops.

Oddballs

In 1812, at Aranjuez in Spain during the Napoleonic Wars, the newly arrived troopers of the 2nd Hussars, King's German Legion, seeing their old friends of the 13th Light Dragoons, gave a hearty cheer. This no doubt gladdened the hearts of the dragoons; it also stampeded their horses, some of whom bolted as far as 20 miles (32 km) before they were recovered.

HEAD IN THE CLOUDS

Beginning in the eleventh century, the Church attempted to establish the "Truce of God," which granted immunity from harm during war to clergy, virgins, cloistered widows, the poor, pilgrims, crusaders, and even merchants on journeys, as well as churches, monasteries, and cemeteries, with their dependencies. It also prohibited fighting on Sundays and feast days, on pain of excommunication. This attempt at the mitigation of war was only marginally successful. Nevertheless, it did it help to "Christianize" the nobility, encouraging the development of chivalry, which in turn placed some restraints on a violent European ruling elite.

"Only the dead have seen the end of war"
Plato

PYRRHIC VICTORIES

Winning is all very well, but not if it entails losing one's own army.

THE BATTLE OF ASCULUM

"One more such victory and we are lost." Thus observed Pyrrhus of Epirus (307–272 B.C.) as he pondered his losses after his second victory over the Romans, at Asculum in 279 B.C. The Romans, commanded by Sulpicius Saverrio, who numbered 40,000, came close to beating him, but were forced back. Pyrrhus suffered such heavy losses that he uttered his famous phrase, thus giving us the term "Pyrrhic victory."

BUNKER HILL

Since Pyrrhus (right), other commanders have shared similar sentiments, such as General Sir William Howe at Bunker Hill on June 17, 1775, during the American Revolution. Advancing in tight formation against the American rebels ensconced on Breed's Hill, forward of Bunker Hill, the 2,100 British Redcoats met a murderous hail of musket and cannon shot. It took three attacks before the hill was taken. Howe lost 1,054 casualties, the Americans 140 killed, 271 wounded, and 30 captured.

Oddballs

Poor old King Pyrrhus, he just seemed to have bad luck all of the time. In his last campaign, while besieging Argos, he launched a daring night attack on the city. An old woman from atop a building threw a roof tile down on Pyrrhus, catching him in the back of the neck as he rode past on his horse. This stunned him long enough for an enemy soldier to behead him.

FACT FILE

Major French warship losses, 1792–1800

	Ships of the line	Frigates
Sunk in action	11	14
Captured	34	82
Lost to the sea	10	6
Total	55	102

HOW A REVOLUTION WRECKED A NAVY

The French Navy in the eighteenth century was a force to be reckoned with, led by excellent admirals. Their achievements during the American Revolution were instrumental in the colonists achieving independence from the British.

COMTE DE GRASSE

François Joseph Paul, Comte de Grasse, won the Second Battle of the Virginia Capes, where his fleet of 24 French ships of the line drove off the 19 British ships under Admiral Graves in early September 1781.

PIERRE ANDRÉ DE SUFFREN

Pierre-André de Suffren Saint-Tropez totally outfought the Royal Navy in the Indian Ocean in 1782–83.

JEAN GUILLAUME TOUSSAINT

Jean Guillaume Toussaint, Comte de La Motte-Picquet de La Vinoyère, was a superb admiral whose daring at Fort Royal on December 18, 1779, prompted his English adversary, Admiral Hyde-Parker, to write to him 10 days later: "The conduct of your Excellency in the affair of the 18th of this month fully justifies the reputation which you enjoy among us."

The French Revolution of 1789 changed everything, as career officers, mostly aristocrats, were purged or fled abroad, leaving the fleet in the hands of jumped-up junior officers and even common seamen. As a result, the British Royal Navy would soon rule the ocean waves for at least a century.

TRUSTING TO ANIMALS

When used imaginatively, animals can be useful allies, though they can be also wildly unpredictable.

During the sixteenth century, the Songhai Empire controlled a major part of west Africa. In 1591, the Moroccans invaded Songhai and their army, 4,000 men, were equipped with firearms, not yet seen in west Africa.

In early March, the Songhai Army met the invaders at a place called Tondibi. Both sides deployed with their infantry in the center and their cavalry on the wings. The Moroccan cavalry struck first, but then the Songhai committed their secret weapon. They had carefully hidden a herd of 1,000 cattle behind their infantry, and now stampeded all of them right into the center of the enemy line, with their foot soldiers following close behind. It appeared that the enemy would be trampled to death.

However, the Moroccans opened up with their firearms. The resulting loud noise panicked the cattle, who stopped, turned, and stampeded back through the Songhai infantry. The Moroccans and their horned allies had won the Battle of Tondibi.

Oddballs

Appian wrote of Rome's war against Hannibal: "Then he [Hannibal] tied torches to the horns of all the cattle he had in the camp (and there were many), and when night came he lighted the torches, extinguished all the camp fires, and commanded the strictest silence. Then he ordered the most courageous of his young men to drive the cattle up the rocky places between Fabius and the pass. The Romans fell for the ruse, and hastened to where they thought Hannibal was, only to find they had been deceived, allowing Hannibal and his men to escape encirclement and then capture the city o⸱ ⸱ronia."

DISROBING IN BATTLE

Taking one's clothes off during an engagement is risky.

THE BATTLE OF CONQUEREUI

While in pursuit of the defeated Angevins after the Battle of Conquereui in 992, Duke Conan I of Brittany paused to strip off his armor, and was promptly killed by some enemy stragglers.

THE BATTLE OF CASCINA

At the Battle of Cascina on July 28, 1364, between the Florentines and the Pisans, the Florentines won the engagement. The Florentine soldiers had been bathing naked in the Arno River when they were surprised. However, they emerged from the river, buckled on their armor, and launched a counterattack. Some 1,000 Pisans were killed and 2,500 more captured. Piero Soderini, statesman of the Republic of Florence, later commissioned Michelangelo to paint a picture of the battle. The artist never completed it, because Michelangelo was invited back to Rome in 1505 by the newly appointed Pope Julius II and was commissioned to build the Pope's tomb.

MARCHING ON ONE'S STOMACH

As Napoleon said: "An army marches on its stomach," and since earliest times generals and politicians have wrestled with the problems of military logistics.

SPARTAN IN EVERY SENSE
During one of his campaigns in Ionia during the Peloponnesian War (431–404 B.C.), the Spartan general Lysander, being welcomed to one of the local city states, was presented with many gifts, including an elaborate cake and a fat ox. Looking at the cake, he asked: "What is that baked object?" He was told: "It is made from honey, cheese, and other ingredients." He replied: "Give it to the Helots [slaves], it is not food for a free man." He then ordered the ox to be slaughtered and roasted in the traditional way, for it was fitting "food for a free man."

For the Spartans, only meat would do. They subsisted on pork stew, the "black broth." It was made with pork, salt, vinegar, and blood. The dish was served with wafers, figs, and cheese, sometimes supplemented with game and fish. No wonder they were a grim lot.

RATIONS

SALTPETER

Military cooks added saltpeter to their recipes, not to reduce sexual drives, but rather because it helped preserve the color of meat while cooking.

SWEDISH SCOFF

In the army of Charles II of Sweden (1697–1718), the daily ration amounted to nearly 2 lb (.9 kg) of meat, 2 lb (.9 kg) of bread, plus small amounts of peas, butter, and salt, all washed down with two-and-a-half quarts (2.8 liters) of beer.

SALT PORK

In the nineteenth century, most European armies subsisted on salt pork. This involved cutting a roasted pig into 52 pieces, each weighing 4 lb (1.8 kg), and then packing them into a cask with the salt and saltpeter. The pork had to be bought in November, and required six months' storage in salt before it could be used.

Oddballs

The eighteenth century was a period when armies established massive magazines (storehouses), filled with everything to keep the army in the field. In 1776, for example, the Prussian Army's magazines at Berlin and Breslau held sufficient grain to feed 60,000 men for two years.

Food in Nelson's navy

The popular image of the food in Nelson's Royal Navy in the nineteenth century is hard biscuits crawling with maggots. Actually, nothing could be further from the truth.

The bread room on a Royal Navy ship was especially designed and located to keep bread cool. Hard tack (biscuit) was thrice baked to completely dry it out, and hence preserve it (for up to five years). The baking also made it very difficult for any insects to penetrate to the softer center of the grains on which they fed.

Earlier, in the eighteenth century, only 0.3 percent of bread in the Royal Navy was condemned. This figure is unlikely to have changed significantly by Nelson's time. If anything, storage techniques may have improved.

At the height of the Napoleonic Wars, the Royal Navy's administrators fed a fleet of 150,000 men, in ships that often spent months at sea. Despite the difficulty of preserving food before refrigeration and meat-canning, the British fleet had largely eradicated scurvy and other dietary disorders among crews by 1800.

MILITARY MADNESS

The modern British Army spends more feeding its dogs than its soldiers. £1.51 a day is spent on meals for each soldier, compared to £2.63 for military dogs.

OFFICERS

Whatever the time period, officers have usually fared better than their men. It's a perk of the job.

THE ROMAN ARMY
The typical Roman legionary fortress provided up to 7,500 square ft (697 square m) of space for the commanding officer, and about 50 for each of his legionaries.

THE RUSSIAN ARMY
During the Russo-Turkish War of 1828–29, a Russian Army of 65,000 men took the field in the Balkans accompanied by 6,000 transport wagons, 5,400 of which were to carry the personal goods belonging to the army's senior officers.

BRITISH AND GERMAN OFFICERS
During the campaign in East Africa in World War I, officers on both sides were expected to conduct themselves like gentlemen at all times. On average, therefore, each British officer had 7–9 native bearers to carry his essentials (cigars, brandy, camp stools), while his German equivalent had 4–6 native bearers.

GETTING HELP FROM THE ENEMY

When in dire straits, you can always look to the opposition to help you out.

WORLD WAR I

At the end of World War I, Krupp and Deutsche Waffen, two German arms firms, sued Vickers, their British counterpart. The two German arms manufacturers claimed Vickers owed them money as license fees for the use of various of their patents in the production of munitions during the war. Krupp wanted £260,000, Deutsche Waffen £75,000. Vickers contested the claims. Their case rested on a wartime measure adopted in 1917, which canceled all patents held by enemy nations.

After a long and acrimonious legal battle, in 1926 a British court ruled that Vickers was under no obligation to pay anything to the German firms. However, with peace restored, Vickers wanted to be able to continue to use German patents, and so the firm agreed to make token payments. After years of litigation, Krupp received £40,000 and Deutsche Waffen £6,000. Krupp and Deutsche Waffen were thus paid a royalty for every shell fired by the British at German troops during World War I.

NAPOLEON'S CAVALRY

Napoleon's military defeats from 1812 onward had virtually emptied France of horses by the time of his first abdication in 1814. Fortunately, between his exile and return from Elba, new stock was imported, often from France's former enemies, allowing Napoleon to fight his Waterloo Campaign.

THE *VOLKSSTURM*

Faced with a serious shortage of weapons with which to equip the newly formed *Volkssturm* (German Home Guard, composed of old men and young boys), in late 1944 Eric Koch, Nazi *Gauleiter* (Governor) of East Prussia, authorized the purchase of arms on the black market from Italian partisans, who had a good supply, gained through fighting Germans.

BRICKS AND MORTAR

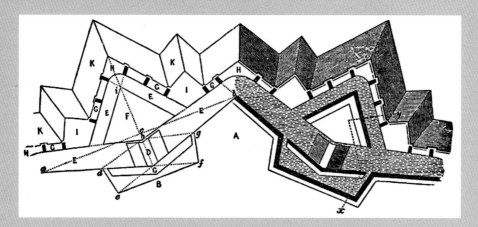

Once monarchs begin building fortifications, nothing can hold them back.

The construction of the Citadel of Lille in France (above) by the great military engineer Sébastien le Prestre de Vauban in 1667–70, required some 60 million bricks and 3.3 million ashlars (large stone blocks) as foundation stones, plus untold tons of stone, masonry, mortar, and earth, for a total mass of materials so great that it proved more economical to dig a canal 12.5 miles (20 km) in length than to transport the materials by wagon.

MILITARY MADNESS

Edward I (1239–1307), the "Hammer of the Scots," was a keen castle builder. This English king spent £22,000 on Carnarvon Castle in Wales, his pet project (his annual revenue was only £40,000). During his reign, he spent around £175,000 on building castles in the British Isles, a truly staggering figure. Despite the expenditure, Carnarvon was never finished and still stands today, magnificent but uncompleted.

PAY, OR LACK OF IT

When the shooting starts, the first thing to run out is always the money.

During the Eighty Years War (1567–1648), the Spanish Army of Flanders, attempting to put down the Dutch Rebellion, regularly ran short of funds to pay its troops. Pay arrears became common, with some units going for years without their wages. The troops were unwilling to desert lest they lose the money due to them, should this ever be forthcoming. Eventually they developed a method to force settlements of their claims: strike

action. Between 1589 and 1607, there were 41 mutinies in the Army of Flanders.

When the troops collectively decided to mutiny, they held a meeting of the entire body—*el escuadron*—and democratically chose a leader—*El Electo*—who was supported by a council of advisors. There were other officials, including a hangman, in case some of the unruly comrades got out of hand.

Some mutinous units took over towns and whole regions, levying taxes and administering justice.

MILITARY MADNESS

In 1793, an Austrian army was forced to surrender to the French at Mainz, because it lacked the cash to pay ferry fees across the Rhine River.

FACT FILE

Compensation claims

Armies are usually reluctant to pay compensation to civilians for any damage caused during the fighting. However, during the campaign in North Africa in 1942–43, in World War II, the Allies paid for any loss of life, or damage to property, that resulted from traffic accidents, using a sliding scale:

In the current conflict in Afghanistan, NATO forces have an ad hoc system when it comes to compensation. The Americans have the following compensation scales (shown below)*

Victim	Compensation (francs)
Boy	15,000
Camel	25,000
Donkey	10,000
Girl	500

Death	$2,000–$2,500
Serious injury	$400–$1,500
Non-serious injury	$200–$600
Serious property damage	$2,200
Non-serious property damage	$200–$250

* All payments are given to family members without inference of legal liability for harm.

SUPPLYING THE ARMY

Before mechanization, armies relied on thousands of horses and mules for transport. The numbers could be staggering.

THE ARMY OF THE POTOMAC

This is a report by Lieutenant Colonel Rufus Ingalls, Chief Quartermaster, Army of the Potomac (below), February 17, 1863 (at this time the army numbered 120,000 men): "During the whole of September and October we increased our stock of animals all in our power. In the beginning of October, my records show that there was with the army immediately present under General McClellan about 3,219 baggage and supply wagons, some 7,880 artillery, 8,142 cavalry, and 6,471 team horses, and 10,392 mules, making some 32,885 animals in all.

"About the 1st of November following, there was much improvement. My records show that, exclusive of the forces about Washington, there were 3,911 wagons, 907 ambulances, 7,139 artillery, 9,582 cavalry, and 8,693 team horses, and 12,483 mules, making 37,897 in all."

THE *GRANDE ARMÉE*

Sixty years earlier, Napoleon attempted to make provision for his *Grande Armée*, but his plans often fell apart straight away. In 1805, for example, his plans for his Danube campaign involved the movement of 150 wagons from his camps at Boulogne. These would supplement 1,000 wagons provided by the Compagnie Breidt. The bulk of the 80,000-strong army's supplies would be carried by 3,500 wagons requisitioned from the areas he was to campaign through. However, the wagons from Boulogne ended up in the wrong place, the Compagnie Breidt only had a fifth of the wagons needed, and locals proved unwilling to part with theirs for any length of time.

MILITARY MADNESS

At the beginning of World War I, the Russian Army (above), the "steamroller" that the Allies hoped would smash Germany's armies on the Eastern Front, was an impressive force in August 1914—over 3.1 million men. However, its transportation system was hopelessly flawed. It faced impossible challenges in trying to deliver the enormous wartime volumes of arms and ammunition over the vast distances of Russia. For example, each bullet fired by a Russian soldier had to be transported more than 2,486 miles (4,000 km) from source to front. And each artillery shell was transported more than 4,040 miles (6,500 km) from manufacturer to gun.

TRANSPORTING THE TROOPS

Getting the troops to the front is a major headache for army planners.

THE AMERICAN CIVIL WAR

The American Civil War was the first major conflict where soldiers and supplies were moved by rail (right). A full regiment, with 1,000 men, 150 riding and draught animals, 12 wagons, and 30–50 tons (30.48–50.8 tonnes) of stores, could board a train and be moving in about 20 minutes. Detraining required about the same amount of time. The troops themselves could detrain and go into action within minutes.

TIBET

Where there were no railroads, traditional methods had to be used. The movement of supplies and munitions for the British punitive expedition into Tibet in 1903–04 (3,000 troops) required 10,000 human bearers, plus 7,000 mules, 5,000 bullocks, and 4,000 yaks.

Oddballs

Complaining that the cavalry was not doing well during the retreat from Moscow, Russia, in 1812, Marshal Murat demanded an explanation from General of Division Etienne Marie-Antoine Champion de Nansouty, who replied: "The horses possess no patriotism. Our soldiers fight pretty well, even when they are without bread, but the horses will absolutely do nothing unless they get their oats."

FACT FILE

The 1990–91 Persian Gulf War

By the end of the twentieth century, aircraft were being used to transport armies around the globe. To overcome vehicle shortages in theater, logisticians turned to airlifts. The U.S. Air Force deployed approximately 149 C-130 Hercules transport aircraft (about one third of its C-130 fleet) to Saudi Arabia during Desert Shield/Storm in 1990–91. C-130 crews expedited the movement of supplies from ports to theater bases (below). The strategic airlifters (C-141s, C-5s, and Civilian Reserve Air Fleet aircraft) flew 500,000 people and 540,000 tons (548,640 tonnes) of cargo into the theater. C-130s moved over half that amount again within the theater.

FUEL FRENZY

Tanks and aircraft are gas guzzlers second to none.

The Allied drive across France and Belgium in the late summer and autumn of 1944, in World War II, consumed about 27 million gallons (112 million liters) of gasoline each day (above). An infantry division required six times as much gasoline as food, and an armored division needed eight times as much.

General Patton's Third Army alone consumed an average of 350,000 gallons (1.59 million liters) of gasoline each day in 1944. In an effort to keep their armies moving, Allied commanders set up the Red Ball Express—a nonstop convoy of trucks connecting supply depots in Normandy to the armies in the field using 6,000 trucks. The problem was, the Red Ball itself used 300,000 gallons (1.36 million liters) of fuel each day. The result was that Allied armies ground to a halt at the end of 1944.

Bradley reported to Commander-in-Chief Dwight D. Eisenhower in September 1944: "My soldiers can eat leather belts, but tanks need fuel."

FACT FILE

Fuel consumption of U.S. forces during the Vietnam War, in thousands of barrels (a barrel contains 35 gallons [159 liters] of oil).

Date	Quantity
1964	2,700
1965	6,785
1966	21,850
1967	36,280
1968	43,650
1969	41,725
1970	36,450

WHEN THE FUEL RUNS OUT

In World War II, Nazi Germany was gradually starved of fuel as a result of the Allied bombing campaign and territorial losses, especially the vital Romanian Ploesti oil fields. As a result, Germany's armed forces ran out of fuel and had to turn increasingly to horses for transport. In France in 1944, the Seventh and Fifteenth Armies relied on 67,000 horses for transport, while in January 1945 there were 1.13 million horses on the German Army books. Meanwhile, thousands of vehicles stood idle due to a lack of gas.

"Two fundamental lessons of war experiences are— never to check momentum; never to resume mere pushing"

Captain Basil Liddell Hart, 1944

WAR IS EXPENSIVE

Killing has always been a costly business, never more so than in the twenty-first century.

FACT FILE

The B-2—in a league of its own

The U.S. B-2 stealth bomber (above) is the most expensive weapons system on earth. Designed to fly undetected through enemy radar during the early hours of a war to destroy key targets, such as communications facilities and radar sites, its costs have spiraled out of control. What's more, given the demise of the Soviet Union and its sophisticated air defenses, the B-2 is de facto redundant. Oops.

Date	Number of bombers	Total estimated program cost	Estimated cost per B-2
1986	133	$58.2 billion	$437 million
June 1989	133	$70.2 billion	$528 million
early 1990	133	$75.4 billion	$567 million
April 1990	75	$61.1 billion	$820 million
1994	20	$44.65 billion	$2.2 billion

F-22 RAPTOR

Not content with spending billions of dollars on the B-2 bomber, the U.S. Air Force is determined to persevere with the air force's Advanced Tactical Fighter (ATF). First ordered in the 1980s at $60 million apiece, so far the Raptor has taken almost 30 years to produce and comes in at $350 million per aircraft, with future orders at $167 million a piece. The original idea was that the Raptor would be able to deal with anything the Warsaw Pact could put in the air. Only problem is, the Warsaw Pact no longer exists. To date, the United States has spent $65 billion on the project.

THE MAGINOT LINE

The line of fortifications along the Franco-German border was started in 1930, and completed in 1937. The Maginot Line consisted of a series of interconnected underground forts protected by ditches, barbed wire, and minefields. It was a formidable barrier that cost around five billion francs. Unfortunately for the French, when the Germans invaded in May 1940, they simply went around it, through Belgium and Luxembourg to the north.

MILITARY MADNESS

King Louis XIV of France (1643–1714), left, spent a staggering 75 percent of his revenues on war. In 1662, there were 60,000 Frenchmen under arms; when he died there were 630,000. It is staggering to consider that while France had less than a third of the population of the Roman Empire, Louis XIV's military establishment at the end of his reign was larger than Rome's. The result was a bankrupt state.

ELITE UNITS

Every general and ruler likes to have a unit of crack troops in his army, if only to protect him when things turn bad.

THE PRAETORIAN GUARD

The Roman Praetorian Guard (below) has a reputation for being a body of troops that idled away its time in Rome, awarding the imperial crown to the highest bidder. Actually, its members were originally recruited from among the best available veteran Italian legionaries. Service in the guard was an honored position, and was considered elite status for a soldier.

And they did their fair share of fighting, especially after the Julio-Claudian era, when enemy incursions into Italy or nearby provinces were often met by Praetorian units. As the deep interior of the Empire was largely bereft of troops in comparison to the frontier provinces, it could often fall upon the imperial guard to secure the interior empire. They also accompanied emperors on campaign, such as Trajan in Dacia, and Marcus Aurelius while he conducted his war on the Danube, where the Praetorians were in the thick of the action.

THE IMMORTALS

So called because their numbers were always maintained at 10,000 warriors, the Immortals (opposite) were at the heart of the ancient Persian war machine. The idea was that when they moved forward to attack, the battle was as good as won. The problem was that they were archer spearmen, armed with two incompatible weapons. They carried no side arms, such as swords, and their defense was a "spara," or large wicker shield.

and Thermopylae (480 B.C.), they were cut to pieces with ease. Still, they looked very pretty.

Despite their desperate pleas, the Roman Emperor Augustus (63 B.C.–A.D. 14) once refused to send troops to assist the people of the Balearic Islands in battling an invasion, perhaps because he thought it beneath the dignity of Roman soldiers to fight an infestation of rabbits!

Their only head protection was a felt cap. When they came up against highly trained Greek hoplites, armed with spears and swords and protected by bronze armor, at Plataea (479 B.C.)

MILITARY MADNESS

In the Bible (Judges, Chapter 20), there is a description of the Battle of Gibreah, fought not far from Jerusalem during a civil war between the Tribe of Benjamin and the other 11 Israelite tribes. The account reveals that the Benjaminites numbered 26,700 men. It goes on to say that the Benjaminite army included 700 slingers. In Verse 16 we are told that these men are all left-handed.

The elite unit of the ancient Greek state of Thebes was the Sacred Band, comprising 150 pairs of homosexual lovers, a measure designed to keep the "lochos" (company) unassailable. It seemed to work: the Sacred Band defeated the Spartans at the Battle of Leuctra in 371 B.C.

OLDEST UNITS

Some formations seem to have
been around forever.

THE SWISS GUARD
One of the oldest military corps in the
world, the Swiss Guard (right), has
been protecting the popes since 1506.
Its most distinguished moment came
during the infamous "Sack of Rome"
by Catholic Spanish and Lutheran
German troops in 1527. On May 4 of
that year, 147 of the 1,899 Guardsmen
covered the escape of Pope Clement
VII from the Vatican.

THE HONOURABLE ARTILLERY
COMPANY
Part of Britain's Territorial Army, the
Honourable Artillery Company
(below) was founded on August 25,
1537. It is older than nearly all active
military units in any army in the world.

FACT FILE

The oldest military unit?

The Roman legion "V Macedonica" traced its origins to the legion "Urbana." Raised in 44 B.C. as a garrison unit for Rome, possibly by Caesar shortly before his death, the "Urbana" survived the Roman civil wars of 44–30 B.C. to emerge as the imperial legion "V Macedonica." The "V Macedonica" had a distinguished record during the Roman Empire. In the fourth century, it was divided into two parts, one of which was stationed on the Danube frontier, the other in Egypt. The history of the Danubian portion of the legion ends sometime in the fifth century. But the Egyptian section remained active on the army list until the Great Romano-Persian War of 603–628, when the Persians overran Egypt in 616–619, making it, at nearly 670 years, the oldest "oldest" unit in military history.

THE ROYAL SCOTS REGIMENT (RIGHT)
Nicknamed Pontius Pilates' Bodyguard, it is the oldest regiment in the British Army, with an unbroken record of loyal service to the Crown that stretches back to 1633. The Royal Scots have served 17 British monarchs and two French kings:
Louis XIII
and Louis XIV.

OLD FIGHTERS

The old ones are often the best.

THE "GRAYBEARD REGIMENT"

During the American Civil War, the Union Army's 37th Regiment of Iowa Volunteer Infantry was composed exclusively of men who were exempt from the obligations of military duty. From the date of its organization, it came to be generally known and designated as the "Graybeard Regiment." Special authority was obtained from the Secretary of War to organize one regiment, composed of men who were over 45 years of age, but who were in good physical condition, and therefore able to perform the duty of soldiers. Actually, a great many of the men were beyond the age of 60 years. Quite a number were between 70 and 80, and one had reached the advanced age of 80 years.

THE *VOLKSSTURM*

In World War II the Nazis, in a desperate attempt to stave off defeat, raised *Volkssturm* (People's Army) units in September 1944. Raised from males aged between 16 and 60 who were unfit for military service, its units were composed of a small percentage of World War I veterans, with the rest being young boys and elderly men (some up to 75 years old). Some of the battalions were under the command of former staff officers who had distinguished themselves in World War I, but were now afflicted with various physical disabilities. The majority of the battalions were short of weapons, equipment, and training, and were never used in combat.

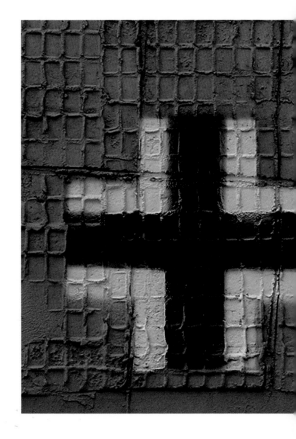

Oddballs

According to the Greek historian Diodorus Siculus, the "Silver Shields," who served as the personal bodyguard of Philip of Macedon (below) and later his son Alexander the Great, were all old soldiers, the youngest being in their fifties, with many in their sixties and seventies, and a few even older. After Alexander's death, the "Silver Shields" served in the armies of later Macedonian kings in Syria and Egypt.

"An army of deer led by a lion is more to be feared than an army of lions led by a deer"

Philip of Macedon

NAPOLEON'S IMPERIAL GUARD

Probably the most famous elite unit in history.

The Imperial Guard was a small, elite army, directly under Napoleon's control. Like a corps, it had infantry, cavalry, and artillery. It was comprised of the best veteran soldiers from every part of the empire—Egyptian Mamelukes, Italians, Poles, Germans, Swiss, and others, as well as French.

However, Napoleon was always very reluctant to commit it to battle, preserving his finest for an emergency.

In this way, he undoubtedly helped his enemies. At the Battle of Borodino in 1812, for example, his reluctance to commit the Guard allowed the Russian commander, Kutusov, just enough time to reinforce the most threatened sector of his line. It was only at Waterloo in 1815 that Napoleon committed the Guard, at the end of the battle, but the British were ready, and the Redcoats stopped it in its tracks. The defeat of the Guard spelt the end for Napoleon and the French First Empire.

THE IMPERIAL GUARD AT WATERLOO

Despite the legend, by 1815 the Guard (right) was past its best. Discipline was poor, the old timers were annoyed, and complained that the Young Guard went out with girls, or got drunk. Hastily assembled, it lacked uniforms and quality weapons (amazingly, not 20 men could be found wearing the same uniform in any company in the regiments). Instead of the finely made weapons reserved only for the Imperial Guard, the guardsmen carried line muskets (musket slings were replaced by strings) and sabers. There was a lack of shoes and food. Supplies were scarce and everything was performed in haste and confusion. The Guard artillery train lacked military drivers,

so volunteer civil drivers were accepted. Finally, the Elba Battalion, who had guarded Napoleon during his exile, looked down on everyone else in the Guard.

FACT FILE

Organization of the Imperial Guard at its height

The Old Guard

Foot Grenadiers (the famous *grognards*, above), *chasseurs*, mounted *grenadiers a cheval*, *chasseurs a cheval*, dragoons, lancers, Mamelukes, *gendarmes d'élite*, Marines, gunners, and sappers.

The Middle Guard

Two fusilier regiments, one regiment of *chasseurs,* and one regiment of grenadiers.

The Young Guard

Regiments of infantry, *voltigeurs* (skirmishers), and *tirailleurs* (snipers). The Imperial Guard peaked in 1814 at 112,500 troops, but by Waterloo in 1815 it was down to 25,870 men.

RENEGADES

Every army has them, though some turn out to be excellent soldiers.

THE SAN PATRICIOS

Before the beginning of the Mexican War (1846–48), John Riley, a career sergeant in the U.S. Army, had deserted with a number of Irish-American soldiers to Mexico, and ended up forming an artillery battalion in the Mexican Army known as the San Patricios. At this time, about half of the regular U.S. Army, and a huge portion of citizen soldiers, were Irish. Irish soldiers despised the San Patricios as traitors and deserters. It was Irish American soldiers who finally captured their erstwhile countrymen, and treated them roughly while they awaited trial, disgusted that fellow Irishmen could so easily cast aside their new homeland and disgrace all Irishmen.

The San Patricios were truly elite soldiers in the Mexican Army, though, fighting with greater vigor than other Mexican units, for the simple fact that Mexican soldiers would be treated as prisoners of war, while the San Patricios would be treated as deserters and traitors, and tried accordingly. This, of course, is exactly what happened. Those who defected after the war was declared were hanged. Riley and many of his men who defected before the declaration of war were whipped and branded. Riley never returned to the United States. He mustered out of the Mexican Army in 1850. His fate is unknown.

THE *WIKING* DIVISION

During World War II, the 5th SS Panzer Division *Wiking* was one of the finest combat formations in the German Army. It did its fighting in the cauldron of the Eastern Front, battling against often impossible odds to prevent the collapse of the line.

German generals were extremely grateful if they could call on the panzer and panzergrenadiers of the *Wiking* Division in an emergency. Yet this unit was a renegade formation, made up of Dutchmen, Danes, Norwegians, and Flemings.

Oddballs

Custer's Seventh Cavalry (right) are a military legend, the 600 fearless, elite troopers who rode into battle against 5,000 Indians at the Battle of the Little Bighorn on June 25, 1876. Custer had bragged: "I could whip all the Indians on the Continent with the Seventh Cavalry." The problem was, the Seventh was comprised of many demoralized immigrants and miscreants, who were also thoroughly exhausted by the time battle commenced. And when the battle was under way, many ran away as fast as their legs could carry them. Poor old George.

AFRICAN-AMERICANS

Good soldiers who have rarely received the recognition they truly deserve.

The U.S. Army's 369th Infantry Regiment, a black unit with white officers, served with amazing distinction in World War I, earning much praise (especially from the French), and setting many records. They served in combat for 191 days in a row, more than any other American ground unit. And they trumped all Allied regiments, in that they were the first to reach the Rhine River. They were cited 11 times for bravery. They never lost a single foot of ground to the Germans, and not one man was captured by the enemy. In addition, 171 men and officers had been awarded the French *Croix de Guerre* by the war's end.

Oddballs

At the Battle of Trafalgar in 1805, more than a third of the crew of HMS *Victory*, Admiral Nelson's flagship, were drawn from outside England, including the West Indies, Africa, France, and Spain (a black sailor was carved on the plinth on the south side of Nelson's Column in Trafalgar Square in London). During the Napoleonic Wars many ethnic minorities served in the Royal Navy, which was a truly cosmopolitan force. At Trafalgar, for example, *Victory*'s crew comprised 441 English, plus 64 Scots, 63 Irish, 18 Welsh, 21 Americans, 9 West Indians, 7 Dutch, 6 Swedes, 4 Italians, 4 Maltese, 3 Norwegians, 3 Germans, 3 Shetlanders, 3 French, 2 Channel Islanders, 2 Swiss, 2 Portuguese, 2 Danes, 2 Indians, 1 Russian, 1 Brazilian, 1 Manxman, and 1 African volunteer.

NISEI

Americans of Japanese descent who proved their worth in World War II.

Despite prejudice, the Japanese-American soldiers of the 100th/442nd Regimental Combat Team became the most decorated unit of its size in American military history. The unit was Nisei (second-generation Japanese in America), but most officers were white.

The 100th/442nd garnered more than 18,000 medals in World War II. The decorations included seven Presidential Unit Citations, 9,486 Purple Hearts, 52 Distinguished Service Crosses, and a Medal of Honor, which was posthumously awarded to Private First Class Sadao Munemori for heroism in Italy in 1945. In 2000, a review of records led to 20 members of the 100th/442nd having their Distinguished Service Crosses upgraded to Medals of Honor.

In the Pacific theater, Nisei "cave flushers" (above) were effective in convincing individual Japanese to surrender, not only because they could speak the language of the civilians who retreated for safety inside deep caverns, but simply by their presence. Japanese soldiers had been told, and believed, that the United States had executed all Japanese immigrants at the outbreak of World War II in retaliation for Pearl Harbor. The appearance of a Japanese face in an American uniform was the first step in discrediting such reports. Cave flushers repeatedly entered the caverns to speak to civilians in their native tongue, coaxing them to safety.

THE WAFFEN-SS

Racial elite of the Third Reich? Actually, a motley collection of anyone the Germans could find to fight for them.

The Waffen-SS (right), the armed wing of the dreaded SS organization, was supposedly full of Aryan super soldiers—blonde, blue-eyed athletes ready to defend Nazi racial purity against pollution by "lesser" races, who the Nazis described as *untermenschen* (sub-humans). Well, that was the theory. The reality was that as the tide of war turned against the Nazis, anyone who had two arms and legs and could fire a gun could join the Waffen-SS. This included many groups Nazi ideology considered to be unfit to serve in the Waffen-SS, including Bosnian Muslims, Albanians, Hungarians, Ukrainians, Uzbeks, and even Russians.

FACT FILE

Racially suspect Waffen-SS divisions

Title	Recruits
13th SS Division *Handschar*	Bosnian Muslims
21st SS Division *Skanderbeg*	Albanian Muslims
23rd SS Division *Kama*	Croat Muslims and Christians
29th Division of the SS (*Kaminsky* Brigade)	Russians
Dirlewanger Brigade	military criminals

MILITARY MADNESS

When the Germans invaded the Soviet Union in June 1941, many nationalities inside the USSR initially welcomed the Nazis as liberators, especially in the Ukraine. But the Germans had come to conquer, not liberate. Hitler's aim in the East during World War II was very clear—acquiring *Lebensraum* (living space) in the East. These lands were occupied by groups that Hitler and Nazism despised: Slavs and Jews, many of them Bolsheviks. Under the New Order, these peoples would either become slaves or would be exterminated. Very soon SS death squads were killing all and sundry (below). The Germans thus turned the indigenous population, a vast pool of potential recruits, into an army of enemies.

AMAZONS

Fierce women armed with weapons may send a shiver down every man's spine, but the truth is far worse—they actually existed.

In ancient Greek mythology, the Amazons (below) were a group of women warriors who lived on the island of Lemnos.

THE LEGION OF DEATH

In Russia, the 1st Battalion of the Women's Legion of Death was organized from hundreds of volunteers in May 1917. Led by Colonel Maria "Yashka" Bochkareva, the women were shaved bald and given modified men's uniforms. They were called the Legion of Death, because each member supposedly carried potassium cyanide to be used to commit suicide in the event of capture. They were disbanded in December 1917.

"*How wise you were to bring your women into your military*"

Albert Speer to Lieutenant General Ira C. Eaker, after World War II

THE "NIGHT WITCHES"

In World War II, the Soviets trained 1,000 women aviators as military pilots, 30 of them being awarded the Gold Star of a Hero of the Soviet Union for their heroism in combat. Three aviation regiments, the 586th Women's Fighter Regiment, the 587th Women's Bomber Regiment, and the 588th Women's Night Bomber Regiment (the so-called "Night Witches"), were staffed by women pilots, engineers, and mechanics. Famous Soviet female pilots included Lydia Livak, who flew 12 combat missions and shot down 9 German aircraft before being wounded and forced to crash-land. She eventually returned to active service, but was killed in action in 1943.

Oddballs

The Aba Rebellion in southeastern Nigeria in 1929 came about because of outrage at the British colonial government's plan to tax women, "the trees that bear fruit." In protest, Ibo women bound their heads with ferns, painted their faces with ash, put on loincloths, and carried sacred sticks with palm frond wreaths. Thousands marched on the District Office, singing protest songs and demanding the resignation of the colonial chief, Okugo. This protest spread to become a vast regional insurrection, called the War of the Women. The Ibo women's councils mobilized demonstrations in three provinces, eventually raising over two million protesters. The rebellion ended in bloodshed, with government troops opening fire on a crowd of women protesters on December 17, killing 32 and wounding another 31. The protests continued into 1930, before petering out.

WOMEN WARRIORS

When it comes to the crunch, women can fight just as hard as men.

DON'T LET THEM NEAR SPEARS
The ancient Greek writer Aeneas Tacticus urged disguising women as men during sieges, so that there would appear to be more troops on the battlements than was actually the case, but strictly admonished his readers not to let them throw spears, "for they will betray their sex by their clumsiness."

MYSTERY CUIRASSIER
On the morning of June 19, 1815, the day after the Battle of Waterloo, British officers came across the body of a "strikingly beautiful" young woman in a French cuirassier officer uniform at the juncture of the Ohain and Brussels Roads. Her identity remains unknown.

RUSSIA'S WARRIORS (BELOW)
All of the officers in her company of the Russian 105th Infantry having been killed in action on September 9, 1915, regimental nurse Rimma Ivanova put herself at the head of the troops and led a successful attack. However, she was killed, a deed for which Tsar Nicholas II (1868–1918) posthumously awarded her the Order of St. George, IV Class, intended for officers. It was the first such award to a woman in more than a century.

The first Soviet citizen to be received at the White House was Ludmilla Pavlichenko, one of the Red Army's famed "girl" snipers, with a score of 309 kills, who made a tour of the U.S. and Canada in 1943.

The field of Waterloo the day after the battle. Among the dead was an unidentified woman in the uniform of a French cuirassier.

MILITARY MADNESS

Bras for the Danish Army

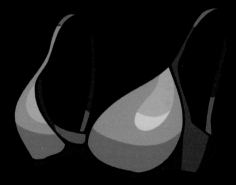

In 1999, Major O.P. Soerensen of the Danish Army ordered 500 bras for his female comrades. However, he ordered them all in the same size—C cup. The manufacturer had assured him that 90 percent of Danish women were of such size. The female soldiers were unimpressed: "But we are big and small, curvy and thin, all sizes," said Lance Corporal Ulla Bekker Madsen.

TOOLS OF THE TRADE

All armies provide their soldiers with weapons, but some work better than others.

Oddballs

The dagger has the reputation for being a weapon of the unscrupulous and the assassin, and for good reason, as it can be easily concealed. During the Middle Ages, for example, it was considered dishonorable for knights to use a dagger, because it was a weapon that could be hidden and then used without warning. This was considered a violation of the code of chivalry.

FACT FILE

Strange edged weapons

• The Sword Breaker—a long and very sturdy dagger that had slots on one side, much like the teeth of a comb, which was used to capture an opponent's sword blade. Once the blade was caught, a quick twist of the Sword Breaker would snap the opponent's sword blade.

• The Triple Dagger—used by fencers. When the wielder pressed a release catch, the two spring-loaded sides came out to form a "V." It was an effective weapon for parrying and capturing an opponent's weapon, especially a rapier.

• Assegai—a spear used in the fourteenth century by Christian mercenaries. It was made of a wooden handle with an iron-tipped point. It was mainly used as a throwing weapon, like the javelin. It was also used by the Zulu tribes in Africa, whose version was shorter and easier to use in close-quarter combat.

• Boar Spear—widely used in Germany in the Middle Ages. It had two wings protruding from the bottom of the point where the metal met the wood of the handle. These wings prevented an enraged, speared boar from working its way up the handle and attacking the spear holder. In combat, the wings could be used to hook and pull the shields and armor off an enemy.

• Bec de Corbin ("Crow's Beak")— a long pole with a pointed end, and, much like the war hammer, it had a hammer side and a beaked side. The beaked side was used for attacking and was capable of piercing a knight's armor. The hammer side was used to knock knights off their horses or to cave in an enemy helmet.

LONG BOW VERSUS ARQUEBUS VERSUS CROSSBOW

By 1500, infantrymen had three different missile weapons available to them. There was the arquebus, the crossbow, and the longbow (mostly limited to use by the English).

Technically, the arquebus was inferior to both the other two weapons in range, accuracy, and rate of fire, while the longbow was generally considered superior to the crossbow.

MILITARY MADNESS

A battlefield longbow was as long as 6 ft (1.8 m) and required enormous strength to pull the tightly wound drawstring as far back as the face, with the other arm fully extended. The shooting range of the longbow was estimated to be 540–1,200 feet (164–366 m). Skeletons of longbow archers are recognizably deformed, with enlarged left arms and often bone spurs on left wrists, left shoulders, and right fingers. Archers' skeletons could also be identified by the fact that some had no fingers — when captured by the French, their fingers would be chopped off so that they could no longer fire arrows.

Each longbowman would have up to 72 arrows, which could last from three to six minutes. However, most archers would not fire arrows at this rate, as the arm and shoulder muscles would burn from the exertion, and the fingers holding the bowstring would become strained.

FACT FILE

Weapon	Range	Rate of fire
Longbow	1,200 ft (366 m)	8 arrows a minute (but archers would tire quickly)
Crossbow	1,050 ft (320 m)	2 bolts a minute
Arquebus	492 ft (150 m)	2 rounds a minute

WHY THE ARQUEBUS WINS

It was cheaper than either the longbow (below), which had to be meticulously handcrafted from yew, and the crossbow, which required equally meticulous workmanship and rather expensive steel. The arquebus could be mass-produced by a foundry in fairly cheap cast iron.

An arquebusier (above right) could carry more ammunition than either of his competitors, which meant that he could sustain fire longer than either a crossbowman or a longbowman, and was therefore able to present a threat for longer.

The arquebus ball was superior to arrows as an armor smasher. Rounded, soft lead bullets were less likely to be deflected by the polished curved surface of armor than were arrows.

Most importantly, a man required considerably less skill to become an arquebusier than either a crossbowman or a longbowman—a few weeks' training. In contrast, it took years to properly train a bowman.

THE MUSKET

A smoothbore, muzzle-loading weapon, the musket entered service in the early part of the sixteenth century. It remained the dominant infantry weapon until well into the nineteenth century. Not bad considering it had serious shortcomings.

FACT FILE

The musket's limitations

• It was long—usually 3.1–4.6 ft (95–150 cm).

• It was heavy, between 9.9 and 15.4 lb (4.5 and 7 kg), and used heavy ammunition.

• It had a slow rate of fire—two rounds a minute (in the mid-seventeenth century, a Spanish musketeer's normal ammunition supply was only 20 rounds, sufficient for 20–30 minutes of firing; he was better off than his French counterpart, though, who was normally issued with 15 rounds).

• It had a short effective range—300 ft (91.4 m).

• Combat statistics show that no more than 15 percent of the rounds fired in battle hit anyone.

• Firepower was lethal only if delivered in great volume at close range on a relatively narrow front. By forming troops up shoulder to shoulder in two or three lines one could maximize their fire effectiveness. If a brigade in line massed 1,500 muskets, it might be able to deliver up to 3,000 rounds a minute. In theory, such a volume of fire would result in around 450 hits being made at ranges under 230 ft (70 m). But as few as six of the hits were likely to be lethal.

Oddballs

In 1817, shortly after the end of the Napoleonic Wars, the British Army had 818,282 muskets stockpiled, in addition to the 200,000 in the hands of its troops. These were the venerable "Brown Bess" muskets (above), which were introduced in 1700 and remained in frontline service with the British Army until 1854. The "Brown Bess" soldiered on in some areas of the world for a decade or more afterward.

WACKY WEAPONS

THE CUDGEL

The cudgel (right) was a rather peculiar weapon. It was for the most part a club, but there were many variations of clubs and cudgels. The most popular type of cudgel was that carried by priests and monks. They were disguised to look like some kind of a religious walking cane or stick, but their real use was for self-defense and clubbing without spilling blood. There were also specialized cudgels that were made just for clubbing the feet of prisoners, and cudgels that were just a wooden club with one end thicker than the other.

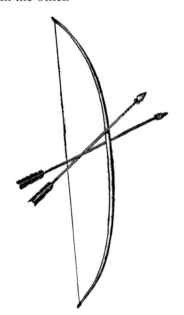

THE LONGBOW IN WORLD WAR II

During the British retreat to Dunkirk in May 1940, Captain John Churchill, an officer who was also a keen archer, carried a longbow as he and his men made their way to the evacuation beaches. On the way, his patrol got involved in a firefight with some Germans, during which Churchill killed an enemy soldier with a shot from his bow. The event entered the history books as the last recorded use of the longbow in combat.

"War without fire is like sausages without mustard"

Henry V

MILITARY MADNESS

"Quaker Guns" (below), used in the American Civil War, were large logs shaped to resemble cannon, painted black, and positioned behind fortifications. Occasionally, a real gun carriage was placed beneath the log. They were used to deceive the enemy that a position was strongly held, and sometimes the ruse worked. During the initial stages of the Civil War, before First Manassas (Bull Run), the Confederates knew that Union troops were watching them from balloons in Alexandria. In order to fool the enemy that their positions were more heavily fortified than they really were, they used "Quaker Guns."

On the Union side, Quakers were used successfully to defend New Mexico's Fort Craig in early 1862. Confederate Brigadier General Henry Sibley withdrew, deceived by the fort's batteries of "Quaker Guns."

POOR SUBSTITUTES

They may seem like a good idea in theory, but in reality some stopgaps are a disappointment.

MOLOTOV COCKTAIL

Beloved of Soviet Red Army infantrymen who hadn't any antitank weapons, and also of long-haired, leftwing students, the "Molotov Cocktail" was first used during the Spanish Civil War (1936–39). The classic is a glass bottle filled with gasoline. An oily, soaked rag is placed in the neck of the bottle. The rag is then lit and the bottle is thrown at the target. However, practice has created new models of the Molotov that improve on the classic version.

When making Molotovs, it is never a good idea to use the oily rag method. It can allow gas to seep from the bottle and many other bad things. The best way is to take a tampon that is soaked

MILITARY MADNESS

During World War I, the British discovered that their standard wire cutters, which worked quite nicely on their own barbed wire, were unsuited to cutting the German variety, made from much better steel.

in gas and place it on the side of the bottle neck. Then, tie a rubber band around the tampon. Make sure the bottle has a cap on it. Light the tampon and throw hard. With this ignition method, the bottle must break or the bomb won't work!

The stickiest mixture is 50 percent gasoline, 25 percent tar, and 25 percent grease. Shake well and throw hard! Think you can knock out a tank? Dream on, comrade.

JUNGLE SABERS

Owing to a shortage of machetes, during 1942–43 the U.S. Army shipped thousands of surplus cavalry sabers to the South Pacific, which proved all but useless in the jungle. They looked pretty, though.

ELEPHANTS

Elephants were big in ancient warfare, being used to trample the enemy and/or break their formation.

FACT FILE

- -

Elephants in battle

• War elephants were exclusively male animals, as they are faster and more aggressive.

• The first military use of elephants probably dates from 1100 B.C.

• The Battle of Gaugamela (October 1, 331 B.C.), fought between the Persians and Alexander the Great, was probably the first time the ancient Greeks encountered war elephants.

• Elephants used by Egyptians at the Battle of Raphia in 217 B.C. were smaller than their Asian counterparts, but that did not guarantee victory for Antiochus III the Great of Syria.

• From the Battle of Heraclea (280 B.C., Macedonian Wars) to the famous march across the Alps by Hannibal during the Second Punic War (218–201 B.C.), elephants were used against the Roman legions.

• In Hannibal's last battle (Zama, 202 B.C.), his elephant charge was ineffective—the Romans simply made way for the beasts to pass.

• At the Battle of Thapsus (February 6, 46 B.C.), Julius Caesar armed his Fifth Legion with axes and told his men to attack the elephants' legs. The legion withstood the charge and the elephant became its symbol.

• During World War I, elephants were used on the home front in Britain and Germany (above) to pull heavy equipment.

STEEL ELEPHANT

The Elephant was the name of a German self-propelled gun designed by Porsche and built by Nibelungenwerke, especially for the needs of the Eastern Front in World War II. It was protected by 7.87 in (200 mm) of frontal armor that was thicker than a naval battlecruiser's armor plate.

Oddballs

Goliath (above) was the name given to a miniature tank built by the Germans during World War II. It was filled with explosives and guided to a target, where it was detonated by remote-control. The Goliath was first used at Cassino, Italy, in 1944, and was also used on the Russian Front to detonate mines.

SMALL ARMS

They may be small, but they they can pack a very powerful punch.

NAPOLEONIC AIR GUN

In the 1780s, a Milanese gunsmith named Girondoni invented an air-powered musket. The Austrian military authorities found, to their amazement, that the performance of the Girondoni air gun was equal to that of any conventional military musket. So, in 1795, Austria began to equip some light infantry units with the Girondoni air gun. It was used against the French in 1795–1800. The Girondoni air gun could be quite devastating in action. The lack of noise made it useful in ambushes, where it tended to be even more effective than those executed with conventional muskets, since the absence of sound made it more difficult for the ambushed to organize an effective response.

When fully equipped, an air gun-armed infantryman carried three full air bladders plus about 120 rounds of ammunition. Each company was supplied with an air pump, a large hand-operated contraption over 6 ft (1.8 m) in height (Napoleon outlawed the weapon when he conquered Switzerland in 1802).

"HIS"

Name of President Franklin D. Roosevelt's pistol, which he kept under his pillow. Eleanor also had a pistol that she carried; it was called "Hers."

THE PUCKLE'S DEFENSE GUN

In 1718, Englishman James Puckle designed a gun that could fire 63 shots in 7 minutes, which was quite impressive in the eighteenth century. Puckle's gun is generally thought to be the first rapid-fire weapon ever made. In addition, Puckle promised that his gun could shoot round bullets to kill Christians, and then kill Muslims with square bullets. He thought square bullets would hurt more!

MILITARY MADNESS

The Italian Breda M1930 machine gun (above) is reckoned to be one of the worst infantry weapons ever designed. The strangest part was its feed system—it had only one 20-round magazine, which was attached permanently to the gun by a hinge. If anything happened to the magazine, the gun had to be partially disassembled and the magazine replaced—not recommended in battle. And reloading the small magazine from five-round clips was slow. The barrel was quick-change, but there was no handle, making an asbestos glove absolutely necessary for handling a hot barrel.

"Dora"

"Dora" was the name given to a siege cannon used by the Germans at Sevastopol in World War II (below). The shell was 31.5 in (800 mm) across, weighed 5 tons (5.08 tonnes), and had a range of 29 miles (46.4 km). The barrel was 107 ft (46.4 m) long and the gun could fire three shells per hour. Sixty railway cars were required to move it. The crew consisted of 4,120 men, commanded by a major general. The gun was sometimes called "Heavy Gustav," and one of its rounds in known to have destroyed an ammunition dump 100 ft (30.4 m) below the ground.

ARTILLERY

Artillery, the "God of War," always makes a big impression on the battlefield.

ONE SHOT ONLY

During a siege in 1748, Afghan King Ahmed Shah's prize cannon fired a ball in excess of 500 lb (227 kg) with such devastating effect that the Persian city of Nishapur surrendered after only one round. Just as well, because the gun itself blew up firing said ball.

THE KATYUSHA

The Katyusha was the name of a Soviet World War II multiple-rocket launcher that was known to the Germans as "Stalin's Organ" (above). Having the effect of 40 mortars, it was invented by Russian General Kostchow from a description of a 10-barreled pistol used in an assassination attempt on Louis-Philippe in 1835.

THE KNEE MORTAR

The Japanese "knee mortar" (Type 89) was a simple grenade thrower used by Imperial Japanese Army infantry in World War II. It had a short, rifled barrel with an adjustable threaded rod inside. Always fired at an angle of 45 degrees, the bottom had a small curved plate to dig into the ground. The Japanese called it a "Leg Mortar," as it was carried strapped to the leg, but a mis-translation in Allied reports led to the term "knee mortar," and the belief that it was fired holding the curved plate against the thigh—guaranteed to break the leg of anyone who did so.

"Artillery decides everything, and infantry no longer do battle with naked steel"

Frederick the Great

ANTITANK AND ANTIAIRCRAFT GUNS

Shortly after the Prussians commenced the siege of Paris on September 20, 1871, during the Franco-Prussian War, the French resorted to the use of balloons to transport passengers, mail, and some specialized cargoes from the besieged city to the provinces. At least 66 balloons were lofted. In response the Prussians developed an anti-balloon weapon.

The *Ballonabwehrkanone* was a rifled, breech-loading gun. Mounted on a special carriage that made moving it easier than a normal artillery piece, it had a 360-degree traverse, and could be elevated to 85-degrees. It was the first purpose-built antiaircraft weapon in history. It achieved only one "kill," when it brought down a balloon just west of Paris on November 12, 1870.

Oddballs

The British 3.7in antiaircraft gun (below) used in World War II was an excellent weapon, and could have doubled up as an antitank weapon, like the German 88mm. But the British military establishment frowned upon weapons being used in roles they were not designed for. The Germans captured some 3.7in guns at Dunkirk in 1940 and used them as coastal artillery pieces. They designated them 9.4cm Flak Vickers M.39(e), and manufactured 100,000 rounds of ammunition for them, for both the flak and the coastal defense roles.

MILITARY MADNESS

The German 88mm antiaircraft gun used in World War II (right) was also a deadly antitank weapon, capable of slicing through any Allied tank with ease at ranges in excess of 6,561 ft (2,000 m). It was called the triple-threat artillery because it could be

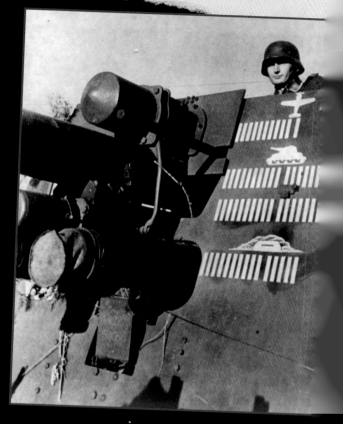

used as an antiaircraft, antipersonnel, or antitank cannon. The 88mm was first tested in the Spanish Civil War (1936–39), where it was observed by a British officer. He subsequently filled out an intelligence report describing its capabilities, but when the report was sent back to England, it was thrown away because the British War Office said the officer had exaggerated.

THE "DOOR KNOCKER"

The "door knocker" was the Germans' nickname for their own 37mm Pak 35/36 antitank gun (right) that was in service at the start of World War II. When battling the heavy British Matilda II and French Char B1 tanks in the 1940 campaign in France, the 37mm projectiles bounced off their thick armor. Similar was to follow on the Eastern Front in 1941, where the gun's shells also bounced off the T-34's sloping armor. Pak 35/36 crews could still achieve kills against enemy tanks, but had to wait for an opportunity to hit the tank's rear armor from close range, a task requiring nerves of steel. The "door knocker" was as dangerous to its crews as to its target.

MILITARY MADNESS

Antitank dogs, also known as dog bombs or dog mines, were hungry dogs with explosives harnessed to their backs and trained to seek food under tanks and armored vehicles. By doing so, a detonator (usually a small wooden lever) would go off, triggering the explosives, and damaging or destroying the military vehicle (and, of course, killing the dog).

The dogs were employed by the Soviet Union during World War II for use against German tanks. The dogs were kept without rations for a few days, then trained to find food under a tank. Once trained, the dogs were fitted with an explosive charge and set loose into a field of oncoming German tanks and other tracked vehicles. When the dog went underneath the tank—where there was less armor—the charge would detonate and damage the enemy vehicle.

According to Soviet sources (not the most reliable), the antitank dogs were successful at disabling 300 German tanks. They were enough of a problem to the Nazi advance that the Germans were compelled to take measures against them. Orders were dispatched that every German soldier should shoot any dogs on sight. Eventually the Germans used tank-mounted flamethrowers to ward off the dogs.

In 1942, one attack of the antitank dogs went seriously awry when a large contingent ran amok, endangering everyone in the battle and forcing the retreat of a Soviet division. Soon afterward the dogs were withdrawn from service. Training of antitank dogs continued until 1996, though.

ALL AT SEA

A life on the ocean waves can be fraught with excitement, danger, and the downright ridiculous.

THE USS *MONITOR*

The *Monitor* was a revolutionary warship that fought in the American Civil War. Its most innovative feature was her revolving turret, the *Monitor* being the first warship to use the invention successfully.

The turret rested amidships of the vessel, and was furnished with a separate steam engine that propelled it in a complete rotation. It measured 20 ft (6 m) in diameter and 9 ft (2.7 m) in height, and its armored

walls were made of eight layers of 1 in (25.4 mm) armor plate. Two massive 11in Dahlgren smoothbore guns, capable of firing solid shot weighing 180 lb (81.8 kg), were installed inside the turret.

The *Monitor* was the first warship to have flush toilets.

The *Monitor* had an extremely low profile—only 18 in (457 mm) of the deck was visible above the water line. This meant that the only target an enemy had when firing on the *Monitor* was her heavily armored turret and the low iron pilot house on the forward section of the deck.

Not a single man aboard the *Monitor* was killed during the famous four-hour-long duel between the ironclads USS *Monitor* and CSS *Virginia* on March 9, 1862, during the American Civil War.

Though she foundered in Force 7 winds off Cape Hatteras on December 31, 1862 (opposite), the USS *Monitor*, which had been commissioned on March 25, 1862, was not officially "out of commission" until nearly 91 years later, on September 30, 1951.

Oddballs

During the long years of peace that followed the Battle of Trafalgar (1805), the British Royal Navy neglected gunnery practice and instead concentrated on spit and polish. Indeed, gunnery practice was actively discouraged by many captains in case the smoke dirtied the ship's paintwork. In addition, watertight doors were polished so rigorously that they became unfit for their original purpose. This neglect of gunnery skills would become painfully apparent in World War I.

SPIT POLISH

YOUNGEST ADMIRALS

Usually admirals are crusty 70 year olds, but there are exceptions to the rule.

ARTHUR HEZLET

Vice Admiral Sir Arthur Hezlet was a World War II submarine ace, later appointed the Royal Navy's youngest captain at 36 and its youngest admiral at 45. On September 23, 1944, off Penang in the Straits of Malacca, he sank the German submarine *U-859*. With a second U-boat lurking, Hezlet attacked and hit *U-859*. He took 10 German prisoners from the water before diving. As he was closing the hatch, a frightened face appeared, and an 11th German politely said: "Wait for me, please." Hezlet saved him, too.

DAVID BEATTY

Admiral Sir David Beatty (right), Royal Navy, was promoted to rear admiral on January 1, 1910. He was just under 39 years old at the time, the youngest admiral for over 100 years, and only a few months older than Horatio Nelson had been when he was created rear admiral in 1799, aged just 38.

RUSSELL ZUMWALT

Elmo Russell Zumwalt, Jr., U.S. Navy, was, at age 44, the youngest officer ever promoted to rear admiral, in 1964. Aged 49, he became the youngest four-star admiral in U.S. naval history, and the youngest to serve as Chief of Naval Operations.

"There seems to be something wrong with our bloody ships today"

Admiral Sir David Beatty at the Battle of Jutland, May 31, 1916

ADMIRALS WHO WERE ALSO GENERALS

In the seventeenth century, some generals also commanded naval fleets at sea.

ROBERT BLAKE (1599–1657) (right) was a general on the side of Parliament during the English Civil War, and later was made a General at Sea. During the 1650s, he had success against both Holland and Spain, enhancing the reputation of the English Navy.

PRINCE RUPERT (1619–82), (below) was a dashing Cavalier cavalry commander during the English Civil War. Afterward he led a squadron of Royalist ships in the English Channel, Mediterranean, and Caribbean.

Oddballs

France, out to recapture the island of Minorca from Britain, sent a fleet under the command of Admiral la Galissonière. In reply, 10 warships in decaying condition, under the command of British Admiral John Byng, sailed from Spithead on April 7, 1756. On May 20, the two fleets engaged in battle. Byng, outgunned and outnumbered in both ships and men, abandoned the island of Minorca and its garrison. To save face, the British authorities needed a scapegoat for the fiasco, and so they had Byng court-martialled and shot for failing to do "his utmost to defeat the French fleet."

NAVAL BATTLES

Where fleets slug it out to see who will rule the waves.

THE BATTLE OF DAN-NO-URA

Measured by the number of ships engaged, the Battle of Dan-no-ura, near Shimonoseki in Japan, in 1185, was probably the greatest naval battle ever. Some 700 vessels of the Minamoto clan defeated 500 ships of the Taira clan. The battle was fought with bows and arrows from ship to ship, and hand-to-hand combat after boarding enemy ships. Rather than living a life of

MILITARY MADNESS

At the Battle of Navarino on October 20, 1827 (right), a combined British, French, and Russian fleet annihilated a Turkish-Egyptian one, in the last great battle of the age of sail. Curiously, the battle happened to take place when these nations were all officially at peace. Not so peaceful for the 3,180 sailors who were killed in the battle, though.

Navarino took place on the anniversary of the memorable naval Battle of Salamis, 480 B.C., when the invading Persian army of Xerxes was defeated by the dishonor, many defeated Taira nobles committed suicide by jumping into the sea and drowning themselves.

THE BATTLE OF FOCHIES
In 1649, a Venetian fleet, composed largely of English and Dutch mercenary warships, forced its way past coastal batteries to enter the anchorage at Fochies in the Aegean Sea, where it annihilated a Turkish fleet, which was itself composed largely of English and Dutch mercenary warships.

THE BATTLE OF MIDWAY
During the Battle of Midway (June 4–7, 1942), one dud U.S. torpedo proved of value to the Japanese Navy, as some sailors from the carrier *Kaga* (opposite) survived the battle by clinging to it as it floated amid the wreckage.

Greeks; and on the same day Euripides, the Greek tragic poet, was born. The battle took place on the eve of the anniversary of the Battle of Trafalgar, in which British victory Admiral Codrington, the British vice admiral at Navarino, then captain of *Orient*, had fought.

SUNK BY THE WIND

It's so unfair when the elements, not the enemy, send you to the bottom.

THE *MARY ROSE*

On July 19, 1545, the *Mary Rose* (right), overloaded with soldiers, was part of an English fleet that sailed out of Portsmouth to fight the French. She fired one broadside, and was turning to fire the other broadside when she was caught by a gust of wind, which made her heel over. Water flooded into her open gun ports, and the ship suddenly capsized, in full view of Henry VIII, watching from the shore.

THE *VASA*

In August 1628, the Swedish *Vasa* capsized on her maiden voyage. She had set sail from Stockholm, steering eastward toward open seas. A gust of wind from the south caused her to heel somewhat. The *Vasa* soon came into more open water and the wind increased in force. A few gusts of wind made her heel alarmingly to port and water began pouring through the lower gun ports. Efforts by the crew to right her failed, and she rapidly sank.

Oddballs

The largest warship to disappear without trace is the USS *Cyclops*, the U.S. Navy's second ship of that name. A 19,360-ton (19,670-tonne) collier, the *Cyclops* entered service in 1917, and continued carrying coal and other cargo to facilitate the U.S. Navy's wartime operations. In early March 1918, while returning from a voyage to Brazil, the *Cyclops* disappeared with all hands. Her wreck has never been found, and the cause of her loss remains unknown.

THE EXPLODING WARSHIP THAT STARTED A WAR

In January 1898, the USS *Maine* (right) was sent from Key West, Florida, to Havana, Cuba, to protect U.S. interests. Three weeks later, at 21:40 hours on February 15, while lying in Havana harbor, she was sunk by a heavy explosion that disintegrated the forward third of the ship—266 men died. An investigation concluded that the tragedy was self-inflicted, probably the result of a coal bunker fire that ignited the forward ammunition magazines. At the time of the incident, the Spanish were held responsible by the U.S. public for causing the explosion, possibly by using a naval mine, and the Spanish-American War began in April 1898.

MILITARY MADNESS

In 1803, British Admiral Sir Samuel Hood noticed the interesting location of a rugged cone-shaped islet that stood barely a mile off the French-controlled Caribbean island of Martinique. He captured it, and commissioned the rocky outcrop as a sloop-of-war in the Royal Navy, naming it HMS *Diamond Rock*. Napoleon ordered its capture. A large French Toulon squadron, under Admiral Pierre Charles Villeneuve, reached Martinique on May 14, 1805. Determined to capture the place, Villeneuve assigned two ships-of-the-line, three frigates, several gunboats, and French troops to the task. Finally, on June 6, out of ammunition and water, the small garrison surrendered.

MILITARY MADNESS

In 1915, a number of British submarines bravely slipped through the Dardanelles and operated in the Sea of Marmara in support of the Allied landings on the Gallipoli Peninsula. *E-11*, captained by Lieutenant Commander Martin Dunbar-Nasmith, while on patrol near the port of Rodesto, came upon an old paddle wheel steamer ladened with munitions and horses. Considering the target unworthy of an expensive torpedo, and lacking a deck gun, Dunbar-Nasmith decided to engage the target with rifle fire. As *E-11* approached the Turkish ship, which was by then close inshore, her crew opened up.

SUBMARINE WARFARE

Only the seriously mad would want to serve in a submarine.

SUNK BY A TRUCK
In World War I, German submarine *U-38* sank a British merchant ship in a surface attack, only to be herself sunk when the sinking vessel exploded, propelling a truck that was being carried as cargo onto the U-boat's deck.

RED SUBS
Although the Soviet Union had 289 submarines in commission during World War II (below), they were able to sink only 128 enemy vessels, in the process losing 110 of their subs.

A squadron of Turkish cavalrymen (left) who chanced to be riding along the shore nearby spotted the engagement. Putting spurs to horse, the troopers charged along the beach, deployed, and subjected *E-11* to heavy rifle fire. Outgunned, and perhaps fearful for his boat's fragile hull, Dunbar-Nasmith broke off the action and retired out of gunshot range. *E-11* was the first—and so far the only—submarine ever to lose an engagement to cavalry.

PLAIN BAD LUCK

On July 24, 1943, the German submarine *U-459* shot down an RAF Wellington bomber in the Bay of Biscay, which proceeded to crash onto the boat's deck, with the result that the aircraft's depth charges detonated, causing the submarine to sink.

THE U-BOAT THREAT

Fears that light reflecting off the gilded dome of the Massachusetts State House, Boston, might provide German U-boats with a navigational aid led to it being painted gray during World War II. The paint was not removed until 1948.

THE CUTIE & THE *GRAYLING*

Cutie was the name of an acoustical torpedo developed by the U.S Navy, which could home in on noise from a ship, and which was fired by submarines. Cutie was copied from a German acoustic torpedo. It was believed that the torpedo had to be fired from a depth of at least 150 ft (45.7 m) so that it would not return to the noise of the submarine. It was first used by Captain Carter Bennett on the USS *Sea Owl* to sink a small Japanese patrol craft in the Yellow Sea. A disadvantage to its use was that it could only be fired at a target traveling at 8.5 knots.

Spare a thought for the USS *Grayling* (below), a submarine that was

"*I cannot, if I am in the field of glory, be kept out of sight*"

Admiral Horatio Nelson, 1797

Oddballs

In preparation for his invasion of England in 1066, Duke William of Normandy ordered specially built transports for his army's 3,000 or 4,000 horses, so that they could immediately go into battle upon landing on the English beaches. An early instance of vessels specialized for amphibious warfare—the first landing craft for horses.

attacked on June 7, 1942, by 12 U.S. B-17 Flying Fortress bombers based on the island of Midway, even though the submarine had given the proper recognition signal. The *Grayling* submerged and survived. When the happy bomber crews returned to Midway with empty bomb bays, they claimed they had sunk a Japanese cruiser.

NAVAL NONSENSE

Wanting to make an unsinkable aircraft carrier in World War II, the British came up with the Habbakuk. Constructed from ice, the plan was to make it 2,000 ft (610 m) long, with a deck-to-keel depth of 200 ft (61 m) and walls 40 ft (12.1 m) thick. It would displace two million tons (2.03 million tonnes).

When ice proved to be not entirely feasible a material from which to build an aircraft carrier, they switched to something called Pykrete, which was ice and wood pulp. A small version was constructed in Canada that weighed 1,000 tons (1,016 tonnes) and was only 60 ft (18.2 m) long. The real thing would take 8,000 people and eight months to finish, and was thus too expensive. Shame.

HEROES

When it comes to heroes, the Royal Navy (right) wins hands down. After all, it's had a lot of practice.

At the Battle of the Nile on August 1, 1798 (below), Admiral Horatio Nelson, standing on his quarter-deck, was struck on the head by a piece of flying shot. The fragment cut his brow to the bone, above an old wound, and a flap of flesh, falling down over his good eye, accompanied by profuse bleeding, blinded him. He was carried down to the cockpit, where the surgeon worked among the mangled

OUR NAVY

Admiral Lord Nelson. "MY SHIPS HAVE PASSED AWAY, BUT THE SPIRIT OF MY MEN REMAINS."

bodies by the dim light of a lantern, but, as he turned to attend the admiral, Nelson ordered: "No, I will take my turn with my brave fellows." The surgeon later found that the wound was not serious, the splinter having slashed his scalp to the skull, causing concussion.

Not to be outdone by this bravado, at the same battle a British gunner was about fire his gun when his right arm was taken off by a French cannonball, whereupon he snatched the match from the deck with his left hand, fired the gun, and then reported to sick bay.

YOU CAN'T KEEP A GOOD SHIP DOWN

The Italian battleship *Conte di Cavour* was the only battleship that was not only sunk three times, but also salvaged three times. On the night of November 11, 1940, *Conte di Cavour* was in company with several other Italian battleships in Taranto Harbor, when a squadron of Royal Navy Swordfish torpedo-bombers flying from HMS *Illustrious* put a torpedo into her, causing her to settle on the bottom of the shallow anchorage. She was shortly raised and towed to Trieste, where repairs were begun.

Then, on the night of September 9, 1943, Italy having concluded an armistice with the Allies, *Conte di Cavour* was scuttled in shallow water to prevent her capture by the Germans. The Germans seized the sunken vessel, raised her, and commenced desultory repairs. These were not yet completed when American heavy bombers once again sank her, on February 15, 1945.

Amazingly, in 1946, after the war, *Conte di Cavour* was raised once again, shortly to be towed to a breaker's yard, and there scrapped.

OLD SAILORS

These are the oldest of old sea dogs.

NAPOLEONIC WARSHIP SUNK BY THE *LUFTWAFFE*

HMS *Wellesley*, a Royal Navy 74-gun ship launched in 1815, was the last ship-of-the-line to be lost in action, when she was sunk by a *Luftwaffe* bomb in 1940.

SOLDIERING ON

Although France scrapped her last wooden ship-of-the-line in 1883, one managed to survive until 1947, when the Royal Navy honorably scuttled HMS *Implacable*, formerly the 74-gun *Duguay-Trouin*, captured in 1805 during the Napoleonic Wars.

AN OLD LADY

Today, the oldest aircraft carrier in use in the world is the Indian Navy's INS *Viraat*, launched as the Royal Navy's HMS *Hermes* in 1953 and commissioned in 1959.

"No gallant action was ever accomplished without danger"

Admiral John Paul Jones, 1778

DOLPHINS

The U.S. Navy explored the possibilities of using marine mammals in the early 1960s, when military researchers noticed how sea mammals' highly developed senses, such as the dolphins' sonar, could be exploited to locate mines and do other underwater tasks. The dolphins were used in the 1970s during the Vietnam War. In the late 1980s, six navy dolphins patrolled Bahrain harbor to protect U.S. ships from enemy swimmers and mines. They also were used to escort Kuwaiti oil tankers through potentially dangerous waters. In 1989, the U.S. Navy started the Cetacean Intelligence Mission. They fitted dolphins with harnesses and electrodes, and taught them to protect Trident submarines in harbor. They were also taught to avoid touching mines, which might cause them to explode.

Oddballs

Oscar was a black cat rescued from the German battleship *Bismarck* by British sailors in 1941 when it was sunk. Oscar was on board the destroyer HMS *Cossack* when it was sunk in 1941, and was again rescued. Oscar was then saved when on the carrier HMS *Ark Royal* when it, too, was sunk.

SKY WARRIORS

Those magnificent men in their flying machines, and other aerial oddities.

EARLY AIR WARFARE

The first aircraft shot down in combat was an Italian reconnaissance plane, brought down by Turkish rifle fire during the 1911 Italo-Turkish War.

The first documented air attack in history occurred at 14:00 hours on July 2, 1849, when an Austrian hot air balloon dropped a 50 lb (22.7 kg) bomb on the island of Murano, near the city of Venice.

In 1848, Venice tried to break away from Austrian rule, so the Austrians besieged the city. They also designed small balloons armed with explosive devices. A preliminary round of balloons launched on July 12, 1849, failed because of adverse winds. A second attempt fared no better. Many of the 2,000 balloons launched exploded in midair, or dropped into the sea. A number even blew back over Austrian forces and exploded.

MILITARY MADNESS

The first air-to-air combat in history took place in May 1808, in the skies above the Tuileries Palace in Paris. Earlier that year, a certain M. de Grandpre and a certain M. le Pique, both acquaintances of Mlle. Tirevit, a diva at the Imperial Opera, quarreled over her "favor." Challenges were exchanged. The two gentlemen agreed to settle the matter with pistols in an aerial duel, to take place in one month's time. Mlle. Tirevit, ever the strumpet, agreed that her "favor" would belong to the victor.

On the appointed day, the two duelists, accompanied by their seconds, boarded identical, specially made hot air balloons tethered 262 ft (80 m) apart in the Tuileries gardens. As a large crowd looked on, the balloons began their ascents. At a height of 1312 ft (400 m), a pre-arranged gunshot signal was fired from the ground.

Le Pique fired first, but his ball went wide. At that, Grandpre took aim and sent a ball through his rival's balloon (which wasn't strictly abiding by the rules). Le Pique's gas bag rapidly deflated, sending him and his second crashing to their deaths on the ground before the crowd of horrified onlookers.

AIR WAR WORLD WAR II

The 1939–45 war witnessed an epic contest in the clouds.

PASS THE AMMO
The "Mighty Eighth" U.S. Air Force (below), operating from Britain, shot down 6,098 enemy fighters during the war, about one for every 12,700 rounds of machine-gun ammo fired.

BOEING'S BABY
A Boeing B-17 Flying Fortress carried four tons (four tonnes) of bombs and 1.5 tons (1.5 tonnes) of machine-gun ammunition for its defensive armament.

BOMBING THE BADDIES
Between 1939 and 1945, the Allies dropped 3.4 million tons (3.45 million tonnes) of bombs, an average of 27,700 tons (28,143 tonnes) each month.

A HEAVY PRICE
In total, 12,000 Allied heavy bombers were shot down in the war and over 100,000 Allied bomber crewmen were killed over Europe.

GAS ATTACK
A number of air crewmen died of flatulence during the war, as ascending to 20,000 ft (6,000 ft) in an unpressurized aircraft causes intestinal gas to expand by 300 percent. Painful!

CARELESSNESS
Germany lost 40–45 percent of its aircraft during the war to accidents.

REAL RED COURAGE
The Soviets destroyed over 500 German aircraft on the Eastern Front by ramming them in midair.

MILITARY MADNESS

During World War II, the German Air Force, the *Luftwaffe*, had no less than 22 infantry divisions. The head of the *Luftwaffe*, Hermann Goering, was zealously protective of these units and often resisted the attempts of army commanders to use them against the enemy. This meant that at critical moments in the war, there were tens of thousands of fully equipped troops standing idly by as the front collapsed.

The Luftwaffe also possessed 13 crack parachute divisions, staffed by highly trained soldiers who were among the best in the world. However, after the airborne assault on Crete in May 1941, Adolf Hitler prohibited any more large-scale airborne assaults (the paratroopers had suffered 25 percent casualties), and so the paratroopers (above) spent the rest of the war fighting and dying as ordinary infantrymen.

HELICOPTER WARS

Despite the thousands of helicopters that have been in military service, thus far only the 1980–88 Iran-Iraq War has witnessed air-to-air helicopter battles, when Iraqi Mi-24 Hinds fought Iranian AH-1J Sea Cobras (supplied by the United States before the Iranian Revolution) on numerous occasions.

During the 1990–91 Persian Gulf War, American AH-64 Apaches (above) were credited with destroying 500 Iraqi tanks, 120 other armored fighting vehicles, 10 radar sites, 10 helicopters, and 10 fixed-wing aircraft, as well as with the taking of some 4,500 prisoners.

"Find the enemy and shoot him down, anything else is nonsense"

Captain Manfred Baron von Richthofen, 1917

VIETNAM AIR WAR

CHOPPERS

Approximately 12,000 U.S. helicopters saw action in Vietnam (all services). U.S. Army UH-1 Hueys totaled 9,713,762 flight hours in Vietnam between October 1966 and the end of direct American involvement in early 1973. Army AH-1G Cobras totaled 1,110,716 flight hours in Vietnam.

WRITE-OFFS

During the war, the U.S. Army officially reported 4,643 helicopters lost in action: a further 6,000 were so severely damaged that they required extensive rebuilding.

AIR COMBAT

Only four percent of U.S. fighters and fighter-bombers shot down over North Vietnam were lost in combat with enemy aircraft, and only five percent succumbed to surface-to-air missiles. The rest, 91 percent, were lost to air-to-air fighter gunfire.

BOMBING "CHARLIE"

In 1965–67, the U.S. dropped more bombs on Vietnam (above) than the Allies dropped on Europe in World War II. Total U.S. bomb tonnage dropped during World War II was 2,057,244 tons (2,090,160 tonnes), in Vietnam it was 7,078,032 tons (7,191,280 tonnes).

Bomb tonnage dropped during the Vietnam War amounted to 1,000 lb (455 kg) for every man, woman, and child in Vietnam.

DEADLY DEFOLIANTS

Between 1962 and 1971, 19 million gallons (71.9 million liters) of herbicide were sprayed over six million acres of South Vietnam to deny communist guerrillas jungle cover. Eleven million gallons (50 million liters) was made up of Agent Orange, which poisoned crops and then went on to poison and give cancer to both Vietnamese and American victims.

HELPING THE ENEMY

TRACER TROUBLE

For much of World War II, it was a common practice that machine guns on fighter aircraft had every fifth or so round replaced with a phosphorous-based round that would burn brightly when fired. The idea was that the glowing tracers would aid in aiming, since the pilot could see where his rounds were going. However, this was a big mistake.

To begin with, tracers have different ballistics than regular, solid rounds. At long ranges, for example, around 80 percent or so missed the target. Worse, tracers work both ways; just as they permit a pilot to see where his rounds are falling, they also permit the target that is being fired upon to work out where the fire is coming from.

And then there was the practice of loading a string of tracers at the end of machine-gun belts to tell the pilot that he was running out of ammunition, thereby offering considerable aid and comfort to enemy airmen. Units that stopped using tracers saw their kill rates in combat nearly double, while their loss rates declined markedly.

SUNK BY YOUR OWN SIDE

The most successful air attack against shipping in World War II was undoubtedly that made on February 22, 1940, by a German Ju 88A of Bomber Wing 30 off the coast of Borkum, in the North Sea, when it sunk two destroyers in a single bomb run, the *Lebrecht Maas* and *Max Schultz*. Unfortunately, both ships happened to be German, a case of poor warship recognition skills on the part of the *Luftwaffe*.

> *"And most of our pilots were lost during the first five flights"*
>
> Adolf Galland, World War II German fighter ace

MILITARY MADNESS

In 1944, the Japanese offensive from Burma into India soon had British forces at Imphal isolated. But if the Japanese controlled the land approaches to the city, they did not control the air. As a result, a massive airlift was undertaken to sustain the garrison.

During the airlift a curious, indeed unique, crisis developed as the 5th Indian Division was being flown into the city. The division had on its books a lot of mules. The latter were loaded onto C-47s transport aircraft. Unfortunately, the experience of flying proved unsettling to many of the beasts. On several aircraft the animals panicked. In their panic some of the mules voided their bowels and, although the solid material was at worst an annoyance, the liquid proved surprisingly dangerous.

Some of the mule urine leaked through the cabin floors, to drip on the electrical wiring that ran below. This caused short circuits in several aircraft. On a number of C-47s this resulted in small fires, which caused several of them to suffer some loss of control. Though none crashed, several of the aircraft were in great danger before their crews were able to bring the fires under control.

CARRIER PIGEONS

ANCIENT BIRDS

The ancient Romans employed pigeons for announcing the results of chariot races. They used them to inform owners how their entries had performed. Genghis Khan established pigeon relay posts across Asia and much of Eastern Europe.

FRANCO-PRUSSIAN PIGEONS

In the 1870 Franco-Prussian War, 409 pigeons were used by the French; 73 returned safely, despite Prussian bullets and falcons trained to intercept them.

NAVAL WINGS

Since radios were too heavy to be carried in the aircraft of the day, during World War I the U.S. Navy provided the pilots of seaplanes with an alternative means of communication—carrier pigeons.

THE WESTERN FRONT

During World War I, over 200,000 carrier pigeons were used by the Allies on the Western Front (below).

BIN LADEN'S BIRDIES

Today, drug traffickers elude surveillance by sending flocks of pigeons, each carrying .35 oz (10 g) of heroin, between Afghanistan and Pakistan. This is a headache for NATO forces fighting the War on Terror, as much of the drug trafficking is carried out by the Taliban.

FACT FILE

Cher Ami, heroic carrier pigeon

In World War I, on the Western Front, on October 3, 1918, Major Whittlesey and more than 500 men of the U.S. 77th Infantry Division were trapped in a small depression on the side of a hill. By October 4, only a little more than 200 men were still alive.

Major Whittlesey sent out several pigeons to inform his commanders what his situation was. By the next afternoon, he had only one pigeon left, Cher Ami. U.S. artillery tried to offer some protection by firing hundreds of artillery rounds into the ravine. Unfortunately, many of the shells fell on the U.S. troops.

Major Whittlesey called for Cher Ami. He wrote a quick and simple note, telling the men who directed the artillery pieces where the Americans were located and asking them to stop firing on his position. The little bird flew 25 miles (40 km) in only 25 minutes through enemy gunfire to deliver his message. The shelling stopped, and 200 American lives were saved.

On his last mission, Cher Ami was badly wounded. The medics worked long and hard to patch him up and he survived. The brave carrier pigeon was awarded the French *Croix de Guerre* with a palm leaf. Despite losing a leg, Cher Ami recovered and was sent to the United States, where he became a national hero.

BIZARRE BOMBS

THE AZON BOMB

This was a U.S. guided weapon developed during World War II. The bomb could be guided by a bombardier, who could only make corrections left or right of the designated course—thus the name Azimuth Only (Azon). It was designated VB-1 or Vertical Bomb, and was first used on December 27, 1944, on a railway bridge in Burma.

POISON DARTS

Poison darts to be dropped from aircraft in cluster bombs were developed by British scientists in collaboration with a sewing machine company during World War II. Military planners believed mass deployment of the darts, each weighing just 0.15 oz (4 g), could be more effective against troops on open ground or in trenches than bombs or mustard gas spray. The "grooved zinc alloy dart" would contain a small, deadly poison deposit in the hollow needle section. Field trials were conducted at an experimental station in Suffield, Alberta, Canada. The project was abandoned, though, when it was discovered that the deadly darts could be defeated if enemy soldiers simply took cover.

"If we lose the war in the air, we lose the war"

Field Marshal Montgomery of El Alamein, during World War II

MILITARY MADNESS

Bat bombs, tiny incendiary bombs attached to bats, were developed by the United States during World War II with the hope of attacking mainland Japan. Four biological factors gave promise to the plan. First, bats occur in large numbers (one cave in Texas, for example, was occupied by several million bats at the time). Second, bats can carry more than their own weight in flight (females carry their young—sometimes twins). Third, bats hibernate, and while dormant they do not require food or any sort of maintenance. Fourth, bats fly in darkness, then find secretive places (such as flammable buildings) to hide during daylight hours.

The plan was to release bomb-laden bats at night over Japanese industrial targets. The flying bats would disperse widely, then at dawn they would hide in buildings and shortly thereafter built-in timers would ignite the bombs, causing widespread fires and chaos. The bat bomb idea was conceived by dental surgeon Lytle S. Adams, who submitted it to the White House in January 1942, where it was subsequently approved by President Roosevelt. Adams was recruited to research and obtain a suitable supply of bats. Sadly, the project never got off the ground.

FAMOUS FLYERS

In World War II, some of Hollywood's finest took to the air.

JAMES STEWART
Stewart (above) served as a command pilot on B-24s, leading more than 20 missions deep into Germany. He ended the war as a brigadier general.

CHARLES BRONSON
The *Dirty Dozen* star was a tail gunner aboard a B-29 Superfortress over the skies of Japan. He was also awarded the Purple Heart.

ROCK HUDSON
Rock was an aircraft mechanic in the Philippines.

CHARLTON HESTON
Chuck was a radio operator on a B-25 bomber in the Aleutians.

JACK WEBB
On another B-25 bomber in the European theater, the *Dragnet* star flew as an air crewman.

JACK PALANCE
Got his looks after a disfiguring accident that happened while bailing out of his burning B-24 bomber.

CLARK GABLE
Gable (below) led a film section making training films. Unsatisfied with this, he then flew on combat missions over Germany where his biggest fan, Adolf Hitler, placed a bounty on his head if captured alive. That's show business.

Oddballs

In World War II, the German Messerschmitt Me 323 started out as a massive glider. The only problem was, the Luftwaffe didn't have a suitably powerful tug to get it into the air—fully loaded, it weighed 99,206 lb (45,000 kg). The aircraft was thus fitted with six engines to make it more airworthy (below). It could get into the air well enough, but it was a lumbering giant that was vulnerable to enemy fighters. This was brought home in April 1943, when 14 Me 323s flying supplies to North Africa were intercepted by Spitfires—all 14 were shot down.

AMERICA'S DOODLEBUG

In July 1944, salvaged portions of German V-1 missiles were sent to the United States, where they were studied by U.S. Army ordnance and aviation experts. By early 1945, they had designed and built an American version of the missile.

The ramjet-powered JB-2 ("Jet Bomb-2") was a subsonic, low-altitude cruise missile. Serial production of the JB-2 began in the spring of 1945, and by the end of July the army had ordered 1,000, with plans to boost production to 5,000 a month by the end of 1945. This was to increase thereafter to more than 15,000 a month, in anticipation of their use against Japan in a massive bombardment that would involve 500 missiles a day. Although hundreds were produced, no JB-2 was ever used in combat.

Oddballs

"Rommel's Asparagus" (below) was the name given to a device thought of by Field Marshal Erwin Rommel to protect inland areas along the Atlantic Wall in 1944 from parachute and glider attacks. They consisted of poles planted in the ground, with wires strung along the tops to set off grenades and mines if the wires were disturbed.

"Air warfare cannot be separated into little packets"

Air Chief Marshal Lord Tedder, 1948

FIRE BALLOONS

Fire balloons, or balloon bombs, were hydrogen balloons with a load varying from a 26 lb (12 kg) incendiary to one 33 lb (15 kg) antipersonnel bomb and four 11 lb (5 kg) incendiaries attached. They were launched by Japan during World War II, designed to wreak havoc on Canadian and American cities, forests, and farmlands. Launch sites were located on the east coast of the main Japanese island of Honshu.

From the late 1944 until early 1945, the Japanese launched over 9,000 of these fire balloons, of which 300 were found or observed in the U.S. Estimates put the total number that made the trip at about 1,000. Despite the high hopes of their designers, the balloons were relatively ineffective as weapons, causing only six deaths and a small amount of damage, and they survive in memory mostly as an ingenious and dangerous curiosity. The bombs caused little damage, but their potential for destruction and fires was large. The bombs also had a potential psychological effect on the American people. The U.S. strategy was not to let Japan know of the balloon bombs' effectiveness.

Cooperating with the government, the press did not publish any balloon bomb incidents. As a result, the Japanese only learned of one bomb reaching Wyoming, landing, and failing to explode, so they stopped the launches after less than six months.

RULES, REGULATIONS, AND THE LIKE

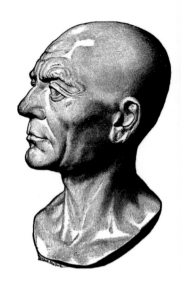

All fighting formations are run by rules and regulations, most sensible, some outright bizarre.

Oddballs

An interesting military custom of the Romans was to grant to their victorious generals an additional name derived from that of the enemy whom they had defeated. Thus, having defeated the Carthaginians, who lived in North Africa, Publius Cornelius Scipio (above) was permitted to add Africanus to his name, while his brother, Lucius Cornelius Scipio, who subdued Asia Minor (though in truth, Africanus, who was his "chief-of-staff," was really in charge), was dubbed Asiaticus. Sometimes an honorific was not awarded, notably when the circumstances, or victims, of the victory were unworthy of Roman valor. So Marcus Licinius Crassus was not granted one for suppressing Spartacus' slave rebellion.

ANCIENT CUSTOMS

THE GREEKS

The ancient Greeks used to sacrifice an animal before battle, and the color of its liver was regarded as an important omen. If it was red, then everything was fine, but if it was pale, then the omens were bad. By extension, the liver of a coward was also reckoned to be pale, which gives us the modern saying "lily livered."

THE ROMANS

The Romans were also fond of sacrificing animals before battle, usually oxen, sheep, and pigs. After a great victory or campaign, Roman generals were accorded a "triumph," whereby the commander and his legions would march through Rome to the cheers of its citizens. Originally, however, a triumph was a purification ritual that cleansed the city and soldiers of Rome from the blood guilt of war.

VIRGINS CAN COME IN HANDY

In accordance with an ancient custom, at the Battle of Korti (November 4, 1820), the Shaigia, a tribe of the Sudan, were led into battle by a virgin, Meheira bint Abod of the Suarab, though her virtue did not prevent them from being defeated by a Turko-Egyptian army.

SUPERSTITIONS

As late as the eighteenth century, military engineers selecting sites for fortresses were wont to "consult the auspices" by examining the livers of domestic animals, not for reasons of superstition, but rather because a healthy liver was generally an indication of a healthy site with safe water.

RANK CONFUSION

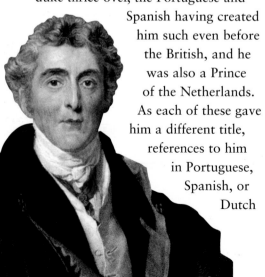

In the Napoleonic Wars, the Duke of Wellington (below) was a field marshal who was usually referred to as "His Grace, the Duke," without his military rank. In Wellington's case, this could become quite complicated, as he was a duke thrice over, the Portuguese and Spanish having created him such even before the British, and he was also a Prince of the Netherlands. As each of these gave him a different title, references to him in Portuguese, Spanish, or Dutch works can easily become obscure. For example, to the Portuguese he was the *Duque de Douro*, and one Portuguese-language history of the Peninsular War nowhere uses any other name for him. Then there is the problem of multiple ranks. Wellington, for example, was a field marshal in the British, Prussian, Netherlands, and Portuguese armies, as well as being a *Capitan General* in the Spanish Army. Although none of the other officers in the campaign had so many different ranks, several held more than one. For example, the Prince of Orange was a Dutch field marshal and a general in the British Army, while the Duke of Brunswick, who commanded his division in his capacity as duke, was also a lieutenant-general in the British Army.

FACT FILE

- -

Many soldiers carry a copy of the 91st Psalm on their person when they go into battle. It is known as the "soldiers' psalm."

1. He that dwelleth in the secret place of the most High shall abide under the shadow of the Almighty.

2. I will say of the LORD, He is my refuge and my fortress: my God; in him will I trust.

3. Surely he shall deliver thee from the snare of the fowler, and from the noisome pestilence.

4. He shall cover thee with his feathers, and under his wings shalt thou trust: his truth shall be thy shield and buckler.

5. Thou shalt not be afraid for the terror by night; nor for the arrow that flieth by day;

6. Nor for the pestilence that walketh in darkness; nor for the destruction that wasteth at noonday.

7. A thousand shall fall at thy side, and ten thousand at thy right hand; but it shall not come nigh thee.

8. Only with thine eyes shalt thou behold and see the reward of the wicked.

9. Because thou hast made the LORD, which is my refuge, even the most High, thy habitation;

10. There shall no evil befall thee, neither shall any plague come nigh thy dwelling.

11. For he shall give his angels charge over thee, to keep thee in all thy ways.

12. They shall bear thee up in their hands, lest thou dash thy foot against a stone.

13. Thou shalt tread upon the lion and adder: the young lion and the dragon shalt thou trample under feet.

14. Because he hath set his love upon me, therefore will I deliver him: I will set him on high, because he hath known my name.

15. He shall call upon me, and I will answer him: I will be with him in trouble; I will deliver him, and honor him.

16. With long life will I satisfy him, and show him my salvation.

RAF RULES

During the 1930s, the British Royal Air Force (RAF) often turned down applicants for fighter training who didn't hunt wildfowl, because, as official documents stated: "The principles of deflection shooting against wildfowl and airplanes were exactly the same," though, "Airplanes could sometimes return your fire."

Strange to say, this theory was spot on. "Johnnie" Johnson, Britain's top-scoring fighter ace of World War II, often likened air combat to wildfowling, and brought to his performance with the 20mm cannon of the Spitfire much the same principles of deflection

shooting which had made him so effective against game birds with a shotgun in his youth.

AUSSIE RULES

It was during World War I that Australian troops (opposite) first acquired their reputation for toughness, determination, and valor, not to mention a certain casual attitude toward the formalities of military life. During the 1915 Gallipoli Campaign, the Australians clung to a foothold on the southwest side of the Peninsula, Cape Helles.

Everything they needed had to be painstakingly offloaded from small boats and then manhandled up the

steep slopes to the troops at the front. The heat was so intense at times that the men stripped down, often working only in their underwear. By chance, one day a senior British officer visited the embattled lodgment. The sight of Imperial troops working in nothing but their underwear infuriated said general. He immediately issued orders that "no man is to be on duty in his underwear." Obedient to his orders, the next day the Aussies were back at their labors, having dispensed with their clothing, to work naked.

Oddballs

From the time he was a junior officer in the Foreign Legion, Achille Bazaine (1811–88), who rose from private to marshal in the French Army during the mid-nineteenth century, always led his troops into action wielding a walking stick. Likewise, General Charles Gordon (1833–85) crushed the Taiping Rebellion in the 1860s carrying nothing more dangerous than a cane. And in World War II, Major Digby Tatham-Warter of the British Parachute Regiment always carried an umbrella in battle. When asked why, he said, "because he could never remember the password, and it would be quite obvious to anyone that the bloody fool carrying the umbrella could only be an Englishman."

THE ROYAL NAVY

NAVY RULES

The Articles of War of the Royal Navy were first officially published in 1652, revised in 1661, and again in 1749. These remained in force until 1866.

GROG

In the Royal Navy, Grog was a mixture of 80 percent water and 20 percent rum that was issued to the men in two daily doses. It had been introduced in 1740 by Admiral Lord Edward Vernon. Nicknamed "Old Grog" because he wore a ratty old grogham coat much of the time, Vernon believed that by regularizing the issue of drink, he could reduce drunkenness in the ranks. He was right, and until the ration was abolished in the mid-twentieth century, it was ever afterwards named "Grog" in his memory.

NAVAL SALUTES

The custom of firing cannon salutes originated in the Royal Navy. When a cannon was fired, it partially disarmed the ship. Therefore, firing a cannon in salute symbolizes respect and trust.

SHAKE A LEG

In the navy of King George III (1738–1820) and earlier, many sailors' wives accompanied them on long voyages. This practice caused a multitude of problems, but some ingenious soul solved one problem that tended to make reveille a hazardous event: that of distinguishing which bunks held males and which held females. To avoid dragging the wrong "mates" out of the sack, the bosun asked all to "show a leg." If the leg shown was adorned with silk, the owner was allowed to continue sleeping. If the leg was hairy and tattooed, the owner was forced to "turn-to."

FACT FILE

Flogging

In the eighteenth century, it was common punishment for a British sailor to be given 24 or more lashes for being drunk on duty. So sailors began to get a crucifix tattooed on their backs. Not only would the bosun's mate flinch from laying his whip on Christ, but it was believed that the lash itself would cringe away.

Flogging was carried out with a *cat-o'-nine-tails* (a whip, usually made of cow or horse hide, with nine knotted lines).

The prisoner was brought forward, removed his shirt, and had his hands secured to the rigging (above). A seaman stepped forward with the cat. After each dozen lashes a fresh boatswain's mate stepped forward to continue the punishment. Each blow of the cat tore back the skin and subsequent cuts bit right into the flesh. After each stroke, the cords were drawn through the boatswain's mates fingers to remove the clotting blood. Left-handed boatswain's mates were popular with sadistic captains because they would cross the cuts and so mangle the flesh even more. Flogging was not abolished in the Royal Navy until 1881.

CRUEL CAPTAIN

Robert Corbet was a Royal Navy captain during the Napoleonic Wars. He was also exceedingly brutal. In just 211 days, from August 1806 to March 1807, while he commanded the frigate *Seahorse* (38 guns) in the Caribbean, he ordered 134 floggings, an average of three floggings every two days. The total number of lashes inflicted was 2,278, making for an average of 17 licks per flogging. His career ended on September 12, 1810, when he was mortally wounded. Corbet was in command of HMS *Africaine*, a 44-gun frigate, one of a small British squadron that engaged several French frigates off Mauritius. Nobody missed him.

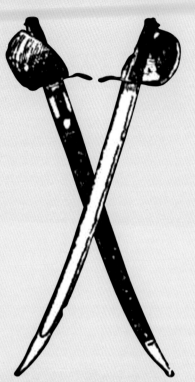

MILITARY MADNESS

Boarding pikes continued as an official item of issue for British warships until 1905. The Royal Navy's officer's sword, first introduced in 1827, is still in use today, though it is not issued to boarding parties. The cutlass was a favored naval boarding party weapon, the last ones being used in action during a boarding by Royal Navy seamen in 1941. Cutlasses were still carried aboard U.S. Navy ships until 1949.

FACT FILE

The Trafalgar Night Dinner, commemorating Nelson's famous victory in 1805 (right), is a Royal Navy tradition, usually celebrated by holding a Trafalgar Night dinner in the officers' mess.

Starters:

Breaking the Line—Smoked salmon and lemon with capers
Cannon Balls—Melon balls
Trafalgar Duo—Roulade of salmon and sole

Main Course:

Fleet Broadside—Beef Wellington with Port wine and shallots
Mizzen Main Course—Roast beef and Yorkshire pudding

Dessert:

Victory Dessert or *Dessert Hamilton*—Poached pears
Hardy's Finale—Cheese and biscuits

Coffee:

Caribbean coffee and Gibraltar mints

After the meal, port is usually drunk and passed to the left.

The Loyal Toast: Diners should stand—unless the company are naval officers, who are specifically authorized to remain seated. The toast itself, by Royal decree, is "The Queen."

"The Immortal Memory" toast is drunk standing in total silence, out of respect to the memory of Admiral Nelson.

DUELLING

Kings and commanders did not like duels among their officers—it's a waste of good leaders. King Gustavus Adolphus of Sweden (1611–32) put an end to duels in his army when he showed up for one with a hangman in tow and promised to execute the winning party.

In 1681, the Emperor Leopold I (1640–1705) forbade the fighting of duels under the severest penalties; Maria Theresa (1717–80) ordered not only the challenger and the challenged, but also all who had any share in a duel, to be beheaded; and in the reign of the Emperor Joseph II (1741–90) duelists were punished as murderers. Frederick the Great (1712–86) also tolerated no duelists in his army.

However, on January 15, 1906, General von Einem, Prussian Minister of War, stated that the principle of the duel was still in force, and Chancellor von Bulow stated: "the army can tolerate no member in its ranks who is not ready, should necessity arise, to defend his honor by force of arms."

Oddballs

In 1931, retired American General William Graves wrote of his wartime experiences in Siberia during the Russian Civil War following the Bolshevik Revolution. His criticism of the aristocratic White Russian leadership in his memoirs provoked a challenge to a duel from Lieutenant Colonel Constantine Sakharov, who had commanded White Russian forces. When he received the challenge by mail, Graves said: "I'll just ignore it. The book speaks for itself."

MILITARY MADNESS

At one point in the seventeenth century, the French Army was losing as many as 120 officers a year to duels, and until well into the nineteenth century, most Western armies regularly lost officers through duels. In the nineteenth century, there was an average of one duel each month between officers in the Prussian Army. The most infamous pair of duelists were two cavalry officers in the French Army named Fournier and DuPont. In 1794, they fought their first duel, after which Fournier demanded a rematch. This rematch lasted for no less than 19 years, as the two officers fought at least 30 duels, dismounted and on horse, with swords, rapiers, sabers, pistols (below), and almost every other weapon imaginable.

THE BRITISH ARMY

LADIES OF THE NIGHT

During the early fourteenth century, English military regulations stated that anyone finding a harlot in camp could take her money and drive her away, after first breaking her arm.

DRUNKEN RECRUITS

Alcohol (below) has proved a great aid to recruitment, though some would-be recruits have taken more persuading than others. When the British Army's 79th Cameron Highlanders was being raised in 1793, a recruiting party billed regimental headquarters for 66 gallons (250 liters) of whiskey, which had been used to help "convince" prospective recruits of the joys of army life.

SLEEPING ARRANGEMENTS

During the Napoleonic Wars—and for a long time before and after—the normal sleeping arrangements for British soldiers was four men to a bed.

PRIORITIES

The British Army regulations of 1899 had 71 articles relating to uniform and dress, four dealing with musketry, and just one concerning field training.

KEEPSAKES

The silver punch bowl long used on formal occasions by the British 18th Hussars (now amalgamated with the 13th, 15th, and 19th Royal Hussars to form The Light Dragoons) was captured from Joseph Bonaparte, the "King of Spain" by courtesy of his brother Napoleon, at the Battle of Vitoria (June 21, 1813), for whom it had served as a chamber pot.

The Byzantine Emperor Nicphorus I was defeated and killed at the Battle of Verbita Pass (July 25, 811) by the Bulgar Khan Krouma, who had Nicphorus' skull encased in silver, so that he could use it as a drinking cup.

Oddballs

The saying "it's so cold out there, it could freeze the balls off a brass monkey" came from when armies used muzzle-loading artillery pieces. The cannonballs were stacked in a pyramid formation, which was called a brass monkey. When it got extremely cold outside, they would crack and break off. Hence the saying.

FUNERALS, LIGHTS OUT

MILITARY FUNERALS

The custom of firing three rifle volleys over a military grave originated in the old custom of halting the fighting to remove the dead from the battlefield. Once each army had cleared its dead, it would fire three volleys to indicate that the dead had been removed and that they were ready to restart the fight, to produce more dead.

"TAPS"

"Taps" is an American call, composed by the Union Army's Brigadier General Daniel Butterfield, while in camp at Harrison's Landing, Virginia, in 1862. Butterfield wrote the call to replace the earlier "Tattoo" (lights out), which he thought too formal. The call soon became known as "Taps," because it was often tapped out on a drum in the absence of a bugler. Before the year was out, sounding "Taps" became the practice in both Northern and Southern camps. The call was officially adopted by the U.S. Army in 1874.

LIGHTS OUT

The British 11th Hussars was the only hussar regiment in the British Army that wore the famous cherry colored trousers in full ceremonial dress. The regiment's last post was sounded at 20:00 hours in the British Army, but the 11th sounded it at 10 minutes to 20:00 hours. This custom stayed with the regiment since Lord Cardigan, a former regimental commander, died—at 10 minutes to 20:00 hours on March 28, 1868.

FACT FILE

Burial at sea (above), a simple yet most impressive and dignified ceremony, is the most natural means of disposing of a body from a warship at sea. It is still the custom to sew the body into a hammock or other piece of canvas with heavy weights, formerly several cannonballs, at the feet to compensate the tendency of a partly decomposed body (as would be the case in the tropics) to float. To satisfy superstition, or to ensure that the body is actually dead, the last stitch of the sailmaker's needle is through the deceased's nose. Ensigns of ships and establishments in the port area are, of course, half-masted during a funeral.

FIGHTING FINERY

It is most important for soldiers to look pretty, even when they are being blown apart in battle. Such a terrible waste of fine material, though.

PITY THE POOR INFANTRYMAN

In the 1800s and 1900s, European infantrymen often wore a neck stock. This was a collar of thick leather, usually 4 in (101 mm) high, which showed at the neck. The stock was buckled or buttoned over the shirt and under the coat. It kept the wearer's head erect and in the correct martial posture, and was always worn with the uniform. But it held a solder's head like a vice, preventing him from turning his head to the side.

The stock had emerged as a part of military dress in the early eighteenth century. The "officers (left) wishing men to appear healthy," used this sartorial instrument of cruelty to enhance both discipline and appearance. They had it deliberately fitted too tight around the neck to make an underfed man's face look ruddy, thus achieving a look of health. But the stock also had the effect of "almost producing suffocation" for the poor wearer.

*Odd*balls

The famous German military theoretician Dietrich Heinrich von Bulow (1757–1806) believed that the optimal uniform for the combat soldier was that used by the Iroquois Indians—a loincloth.

MILITARY MADNESS

By 1943, Albert Speer had become German Armaments Minister. This position gave him the power to determine the allocation of Germany's industrial resources in the continuance of the Nazi war effort.

As it happened, German naval regulations prescribed a decorative dirk—a dagger—as a part of the dress uniform for officers, petty officers, and naval cadets. It could usually be seen dangling from their belts as they boarded

their ships (right). Perceiving a shortage of this vital piece of military equipment, in 1943 the navy requested that Speer arrange for the manufacture of no less than 50,000 of the useless things.

Apparently controlling his temper, Speer turned the navy down, informing it that the metal might better serve Germany's war effort if used for something besides ensuring that naval personnel were correctly uniformed. The navy was outraged, and protested this decision right up to Hitler. To no avail.

CAVALRY UNIFORMS

Cavalry have always worn more striking uniforms, mostly because, as they are physically higher than the infantry in battle, they have more opportunities to show off. And this is still the case in modern armies. Here are just a few of the uniform rules for two British cavalry regiments.

THE LIFE GUARDS (CEREMONIAL DRESS)

The helmet

A gilt metal rosette, 2.25 in (57.1 mm) in diameter with four inner rows of petals, is screwed into each side of the helmet. This secures the ends of the gilt curb chain. It is 16.5 in (419 mm) long and mounted on black leather. In The Life Guards, the chain is worn under the lower lip.

The plume

The plume is fitted to the helmet by passing the stem through the spike and securing it underneath with a butterfly screw. In order to obtain the "onion" shape of the plume, it is tied under the dome when not in use. This is customary only in The Life Guards.

The plume's hair hangs from the mould to a length of 24.5 in (622 mm), and falls below the bottom of the helmet.

THE BLUES AND ROYALS (CEREMONIAL DRESS)

The plume

It has a fluffy texture to the touch, whereas the plume worn by The Life Guards is sleek.

It is fitted in the same manner as for The Life Guards, but a gilt rosette is positioned at the top. The plume is 19 in (483 mm) long, and should hang level with the bottom of the helmet.

JACK BOOTS & SPURS

Officers of the Household Cavalry

Jack Boots are black and plain fronted. Calf leather is used for the vamps and counters, and dressed hide for the legs. The extension on the front of the

Oddballs

French cuirassiers in the Napoleonic Wars wore a long cloak, a semicircular wool cape that ran from the trooper's shoulders down to his boot tops and extending to the horse's hips and croup. When not worn, this cape was folded and attached atop the portmanteau. When battle was anticipated, the troopers strapped the cloak roll laterally across their saddle pommel, providing protection from their groin to the bottom of the cuirass.

legs is lined with buckskin. The uppers, welts, seats, and heels are all hand-sewn, and the soles reinforced with wooden pegs. Steel tips are fitted to the 1.5-in (38-mm) high heels.

Officers of The Life Guards

The spurs, chains, and buckles for use with Jack Boots are of the best super nickel, and are assembled to "V" shape tabs (left and right), which are 2.75 in (69.8 mm) in width, and have buckling straps, which are produced from light hide, and dyed black.

Officers of The Blues And Royals

The Jack Spurs are of the best super nickel, whilst the chains and buckles are of brass. They are assembled to tabs (left and right), which are 2.5 in (69.8 mm) in width, and have buckling straps which are produced from light hide, and dyed black.

Other Ranks of the Household Cavalry

Jack Boots are made of black leather of similar appearance to the Officers' pattern, but not of such high grade material. There is no leather roll above the spur rest, as for Officers.

Other Ranks of the Household Cavalry

The Jack Spurs are the 1955 pattern, and are produced from forged steel. The chains are steel, and are assembled to tabs, which are 2.5 in (69.8 mm) in width, and have buckling straps which are made from light hide, dyed black.

BRITISH REDCOATS

British troops are traditionally associated with red uniforms, but how did this come about?

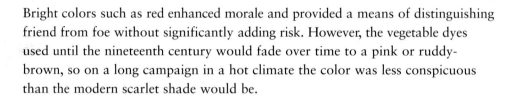

Red was not used in order to hide blood stains—a blood stain on a uniform turns black.

The uniforms of the Yeomen of the Guard (formed 1485) and the Yeomen Warders (also formed 1485) have traditionally been in Tudor red and gold.

In February 1645, when the Parliament of England passed the New Model Army ordinance, the new English Army comprised infantry regiments who wore coats of Venetian red with white facings.

Bright colors such as red enhanced morale and provided a means of distinguishing friend from foe without significantly adding risk. However, the vegetable dyes used until the nineteenth century would fade over time to a pink or ruddy-brown, so on a long campaign in a hot climate the color was less conspicuous than the modern scarlet shade would be.

FACT FILE

The epithet "Redcoats" is familiar throughout much of the former British Empire, even though this color was by no means exclusive to the British Army. The entire Danish Army wore red coats up to 1848, and particular units in the German, French, Austro-Hungarian, Russian, Bulgarian, and Romanian armies retained red uniforms until 1914 or later. Among other diverse examples, Spanish hussars, Japanese Army bandsmen, and Serbian generals had red tunics as part of their gala or court dress.

MILITARY MADNESS

The last occasion on which British troops went into action wearing their traditional redcoats was at the Battle of Ginnis, in the Sudan, on December 30, 1885. In the campaign of 1885, it was thought that if the troops marched out in redcoats, the Mahdist tribesmen would know that they were fighting British soldiers, and their morale and enthusiasm would drop. Many units disembarked in red and some marched out on their first patrols in red.

However, the redcoat was unsuitable for the Sudanese climate. The Sudanese knew, from their earlier experiences, who they were fighting, and only their tactics, not their morale, changed. The redcoat was soon discarded and all British troops were issued khaki.

HEADGEAR

THE STEEL HELMET

The modern steel helmet was first worn in World War I. Its purpose was to protect the wearer from shrapnel and debris. It was not intended to stop bullets. Unfortunately, after the initial issue of steel helmets there was a major increase in head injuries among frontline troops. The soldiers were under the impression that they were immune when wearing the helmet, and began peering over the trench parapet to look at enemy positions.

THE BEARSKIN

The tall British Army fur cap (right) is called a bearskin, never a busby. The standard bearskin of the British Foot Guards is 18 in (457 mm) tall, weighs 1.5 lb (.68 kg), and is made from the fur of the Canadian black bear. However, an officer's bearskin is made from the fur of the Canadian brown bear, dyed black, as the female brown bear has thicker, fuller fur. The British Army purchases the hats, which are known as caps, from a British hatmaker, which sources its pelts at an international auction. The hatmakers purchase between 50 and 100 black bear skins each year, at a cost of about $1,080 each. If properly maintained, the caps last for decades. Some caps in use, for example, are reportedly more than 100 years old.

"Drill is necessary to make the soldier steady and skilful"

Field Marshal Maurice Comte de Saxe, 1732

DRUMMERS

BRITISH ARMY DRUMMERS

In the 1700s, it was the fashion in British Army regiments to employ drummers from Africa and the West Indies. Officers on inspection tours rated these drummers very highly in terms of musical abilities. Major General Sir William Howe, upon inspecting the 29th Regiment of Foot at Dover in 1774, remarked that the African musicians "play and beat well" on fife and drum. The 29th Regiment was again inspected some 17 years later, and this time the inspecting officer commented, very bluntly, that "The drummers, black, beat and play well."

MEDIEVAL DRUMMERS

Foreign percussionists may have first gained a place in British military music in the Crusades during the Middle Ages. A manuscript in the British Museum

dating from the 1300s shows a negro carrying a pair of kettledrums for a drummer marching behind, while playing the cymbals himself.

FACT FILE

On August 18, 1861, during the American Civil War, Avery Brown (1852–1904) was mustered into Company C, 31st Ohio Volunteer Infantry, at the age of 8 years, 11 months, and 13 days. He was dubbed "The Drummer Boy of the Cumberland," until illness forced him to take a disability discharge in 1863. Brown holds the record as America's youngest military drummer boy.

Oddballs

Ancient trumpets were used at religious ceremonies and associated with magical rites. Burials, circumcisions, and sunset rites (to ensure the sun would return) were a few of the early ceremonies in which the trumpet was used. It was a male-dominated practice, and among certain tribes of the Amazon any woman who looked at a trumpet was killed. The tradition of playing at sunrise (Reveille), sunset (Retreat), and at burials (Taps) may have evolved from these ancient rituals.

" Attack is the chief means of destroying the enemy"

Mao Tse-tung, 1938

HORNS AND BUGLES

JOSHUA'S TRUMPETS

According to the Bible, the first big city the Israelites attacked when they crossed the Jordan River into Canaan, The Promised Land, was Jericho. Josuha set his troops circling the city for six days, carrying the Ark of the Covenant before them and blowing trumpets (right). And on the seventh day they circled the city seven times, still with the Ark, and still blowing their trumpets. Then all the Israelites let out an almighty shout, and the walls of Jericho fell down, allowing Joshua's troops to sack the city.

EARLY TRUMPETS

Early bugles and trumpets bear little resemblance to those of today. Trumpets can be traced to pre-Biblical times, being used by Egyptians and Israelites. The earliest trumpets were straight instruments with no mouthpiece and no flaring bell. These trumpets were actually megaphones into which one spoke, sang, or roared. The effect was to distort the natural voice and produce a harsh sound to frighten evil spirits.

THE REVOLUTIONARY WAR

Bugles were first used for signaling in America by the British Army during the Revolutionary War. The sound of the bugle made it possible to convey commands over a great distance and could usually be heard above the roar of battle.

THE KILT

Originally, the kilt was the garment worn by shepherds, the poor, and highlanders who had very little. It was their blanket at night and their clothing by day.

THE GREAT KILT

At the time when the great kilt was worn (1500 to the 1740s, when it was banned after the Battle of Culloden) tartans as we know them did not exist. Patterns were made up of natural colors from white and black sheep,

with some dyes made from local ingredients. The great kilt, also known as the belted plaid, was an untailored draped garment made of cloth gathered up into pleats by hand and secured by a wide belt. The upper half could be worn as a cloak draped over the left shoulder, hung down over the belt, and gathered up at the front, or brought up over the shoulders (left) or head for protection against weather. It was worn over a *léine* (a full-sleeved garment gathered along the arm length and stopping below the waist) and could also serve as a blanket. For battle, it was customary to take off the kilt beforehand, the Highland charge being made wearing only the *léine*.

Oddballs

Scottish troops en masse last wore kilts in combat during World War I (below). The ferocious tactics of the Royal Highland Regiment led to their being nicknamed "Ladies from Hell" by German troops that faced them in the trenches. The kilt was last worn in action early in World War II, in May 1940 at the Battle of Dunkirk. This was the last time a Highland battalion fought in the kilt.

TARTAN TERRIERS

Scottish Highlanders wearing their traditional tartan were drafted into the British Army around 1750. By an English stroke of genius, the bottom part of the great kilt was sewn into a skirt, and incorporated into the grenadier uniform of the British Army.

THE EMIR'S KILTED KILLERS

So impressed was the Emir of Afghanistan with the prowess of Britain's Highland troops in the nineteenth century (opposite, top), that he decided to raise some of his own. So he ordered bagpipes and kilts from merchants in India, with which to outfit his new regiments. As a result, during the Second Afghan War (1879–81), Afghan troops several times went into battle against the British wearing kilts and accompanied by pipe music.

PROTECTION

PAPER ARMOR

The ancient Chinese discovered that pleated sheets of paper could stop the penetration of arrows. Paper armor was standard issue with Chinese land and sea units.

SAMURAI ARMOR

Japanese samurai warriors (above) wore wraparound lamellar armor, with shoulder flaps and skirt. Such protected costumes were worn in Japan until 1876, and in Tibet well into the twentieth century.

GOTHIC ARMOR

The fully articulated plate armor developed in the first half of the fifteenth century is called Gothic, because of its emphasis on vertical lines and its spiky silhouette reminiscent of Gothic architecture. About 1500, the style changed, with the more rounded shapes characteristic of Renaissance style dominant. A variant favored in Germany for its additional strength (the so-called Maximilian armor, after the emperor Maximilian I) had fluted surfaces, like corrugated iron.

"A mighty name will remain behind me"
Genghis Khan

THE MONGOLS

The Mongols wore armor made of scales of iron sewn to garments of thick hide, and iron helmets that sometimes came to a point on top. The legs were often protected by overlapping iron plates resembling fish scales, which were sewn into the boots.

They also wore a raw silk coat under their armor for additional protection. An arrow, when it hit its target, would carry the unpierced silk into the flesh and the arrow could be removed by pulling gently at the coat (the Mongols never abandoned their wounded).

Some Mongols made horse armor in five sections; one on each side from head to tail, fastened to the saddle and behind the saddle on its back, and also on the neck. A third section stretched over the hindquarters and was tied to the side parts; a fourth piece covered the breast; and a fifth piece, an iron plate for the forehead, was fastened on each side of the neck.

FACT FILE

In the construction of Medieval armor, the weight problem was crucial. Armor was supposed to give maximum protection with minimal weight. A full suit of battle armor was not to exceed about 65 lb (29 kg). Such a suit, well articulated and fitted to the body, was expected to give a knight full mobility, so that he might mount a horse without stirrups in an emergency. Tournament armor, on the other hand, was up to twice as heavy, safety rather than mobility being the prime consideration.

ZOUAVE UNIFORMS

The original Zouaves were native North African troops serving in the French Army in the 1830s (below). Their uniforms usually consisted of a fez and turban, very baggy pants, a vest, a short jacket that was cut away from the top, with only one button or clasp at the throat, and a sash. They also wore leggings. The uniforms were usually brightly colored.

These soldiers fought in North Africa for French interests. Later, Zouaves fought in the Crimea War and in Italy in the 1850s. Zouaves were well trained and disciplined, and were famous for great feats on the battlefield—and often mischief and rowdiness off it.

FACT FILE

A unique presence in American Civil War Zouave regiments was the *vivandiere*. They were women who dressed in a uniform similar to the men (right). Many Zouave regiments had *vivandieres* who performed a variety of duties, most notably nursing on the battlefield.

Mary Tepee, or "French Mary" as she was called, was the *vivandiere* of the 114th Pennsylvania Infantry Regiment. Mary was present on almost every Civil War battlefield where the regiment fought, and acted as a battlefield nurse and aide. She carried water and bandages into battle, and was herself wounded during the war.

Mary was present with the regiment at Gettysburg in July 1863 and was one of the few women with the Union Army to ever experience combat. Her regiment, called "Collis' Zouaves," was one of the best known Zouave regiments of the war, heralded for their precision on the drill field. The men wore flashy Zouave-style uniforms, featuring bright red trousers, white leggings, blue jacket, and red fez.

The 114th fought in almost every major battle with the Army of the Potomac. In 1864, the regiment was appointed the headquarters guard for General George Meade.

INDEX